NORTH AMERICA HOT AND HIP
A Trendsetter's Guide

David Andrusia

John Wiley & Sons, Inc.

New York • Chichester • Brisbane • Toronto • Singapore

Recognizing the importance of preserving what has been written, it is a policy of John Wiley & Sons, Inc., to have books of enduring value published in the United States printed on acid-free paper, and we exert our best efforts to that end.

Library of Congress Cataloging-in-Publication Data

Andrusia, David.
    North America hot and hip : a trendsetter's guide / David Andrusia.
        p.   cm.
    ISBN 0-471-52857-9 (paper)
    1. North America—Description and travel—Guide-books.
I. Title. II. Title: North America hot and hip.
E41.A53   1991
917.04'539—dc20   90-44695

Printed in the United States of America

91 92 10 9 8 7 6 5 4 3 2 1

PREFACE

The Empire State Building, Art Institute of Chicago, and San Diego Zoo are but a few of the attractions you'll *not* find covered here.

In fact, San Diego isn't even *in* this book. Oh, I know—it's supposed to be a highly desirable place to live (at least if you're into surf, sun, and sailors), and it may be hot, but it sure ain't hip.

It's a subjective call, to be sure, and I'm still smarting over omissions in my European trendsetter's guide. But as Miss Thomas, my sixth grade teacher, admonished: "When you write, take a stand!" So I am—and that's why Atlanta, Houston, and San Diego (among other North American burghs) are not included in this tome. But I'm not pathologically stubborn; if you feel strongly about the hip quotient of certain passed-over cities, write and let me know.

What I've once again tried to do is to find the heart and soul of the major cities in Canada, Mexico, and the United States. The good, the bad, and the ugly—they're all presented here. In fact, I already have friends in both L.A. and New York who have launched formal protests after reading the chapters on their hometowns. Steadfast, however, I stand by my remarks. (If you're into the sugar-coated, "everything is beautiful" point of view, read almost any other travel guide. What you get here is the hard, brutal truth.)

You'll find more than that, of course—namely, the listings that are the hallmarks of my guides. Yes, I worked till the wee hours of the morning, exploring North America's most glamorous watering holes . . . but for you, dear reader, nothing is too much work. (And if one is plied by constant offers of sex, drugs, and rock 'n' roll—hey, it's all in a day's work.)

The best reward of traveling throughout our continent is finding that one totally unexpected place—a café, a bar, a vintage clothing shop—with which you immediately fall in love. The downside, of course, is that you can't take it home with you—only the memory, one you inevitably romanticize beyond any semblance of its original self. Of one St. Louis club, of which I've oft waxed poetic, a friend shot back: "My God, you make it sound like Madonna and Princess Stephanie were there!"

And which cities do I like the best? What, and save you the price of this book? As I would have teased in Miss Thomas's class: "If you want to know what happens, read the book and find out!"

David Andrusia
Los Angeles

CONTENTS

BALTIMORE

Baltimore is a wonderful example of a city with a vision.

Like most aging eastern cities, the '60s and '70s were less than kind to Baltimore. The urban unrest and decaying manufacturing base led the young and affluent to homes in the suburbs and left the poor and working class with a future that can best be described as dim.

Unlike similar cities, however, Baltimore did not wait until its problems became insurmountable. Instead, city planners devised a strategy to bring prominence back to the core of the city, and the plan worked: five years ago, Baltimore was the 12th-largest city in the United States; today, it has moved up a notch to 11th. Hats off!

The literal and metaphorical symbol of the city's renaissance is Harborplace, the Rouse Company development in the scenic Inner Harbor area. Its shops are
more touristy than sophisticated—though even the
snottiest palates will find something to like in the myriad
food stalls there—but it's a fine shrine indeed to the
renewed city scene. On a sunny weekend day, the mall
and inviting harborside promenade are packed with
families that represent social and economic strata as
varied as Baltimore itself.

Harborplace has also brought renewed vigor to the
entire downtown area, as hotel and commercial con-
struction proudly show. Best of all is the sense of pride
Baltimoreans feel, and the city's clean-as-a-whistle status
is testament to their pride.

Fells Point is the other neighborhood you're certain to
have heard about, key as it is to the John Waters frame of
mind. The Patron Saint of Cine-Kitsch, and his clique of
hangers-on and wanna-bes, discovered the area long
ago, when it was even campier and trashier than it is
now. A former haven for sailors and down-and-outs,
Fells Point still boasts its share of junk shops and dere-
licts, but many of the seamier bars have given way to
upscale restaurants and galleries. But not to worry: the
Point still has a slovenly, end-of-the-world feel.

Few cities anywhere can match the grandeur of central
Baltimore's colonial architecture, especially that of
Mount Vernon and Charles Street. And the Washing-
ton Monument—which preceded, by the way, the one in
D.C.—is a strong and beautiful city square.

As you stray from this city core, of course, the federal

architecture gives way to rowhouses in various states of upkeep and tone. Above all, Baltimore is a city of ethnic neighborhoods; there are many groups, but African-Americans, Italians, Irish, Poles, and other Eastern Europeans are the predominant cultural claques.

Baltimore's cultural life is varied and strong, the hallmark being the Symphony Orchestra that is ranked among the best in the world. Smaller yet secure ballet and opera companies are also in force.

Theater is less varied, but—surprise—Baltimore is a major jazz sound. In fact, many unrecognized locals considered demi-legends play in many of the new and traditional jazz rooms. If jazz is your bag, you'll have a heyday here.

Make no mistake: Baltimore is not Paris, and it isn't New York. But it is one of the country's most under-appreciated cities and is certainly a model of renewed urban pride. It's probably not your dream destination, but if it's on your way, stop off and take a look around. You may well be pleasantly surprised at what you find.

IN TRANSIT

Baltimore is well served by Amtrak's conventional and Metroliner trains. It's very convenient to other Northeast Corridor cities, so much so that it's a wonder more people haven't stopped by for a quick weekend jaunt. (In fairness though, Baltimore's tourism numbers are drastically higher than they were a few years ago, thanks in part to Inner Harbor and Harborplace.)

If you can, don't miss Amtrak's Club Car service, which features excellent hot meals, beverages, hot towels, and the newspaper of your choice. You'll feel so pampered that you'll probably reach your destination before you know it. The Club Car is a strong rival to first class service on the best European trains—but don't blame me if you become too spoiled for less luxuriant rides!

GETTING CENTERED

Downtown Baltimore is easy to get to know and can certainly be mastered in an hour or two. To the south lies the picturesque Inner Harbor, five minutes from the core of downtown; to the east lies Little Italy (and it's *piccolo* indeed!); to its southeast, you'll find Fells Point. And those, basically, are the neighborhoods you'll need to know.

One word of caution: it's only a 25-minute walk from downtown, but you should probably take a cab to Fells Point, even in the light of day. This is because to get there, you'll have to walk through a series of public housing projects, all of which are unsavory spots indeed. Spend the four-dollar fare and consider it insurance. I decided to walk to the Point from my hotel, and met with a couple of very close calls. Understood?

HOTELS

Best Western Hallmark (8 N. Howard St; 301/539-1188) A good budget choice in the heart of downtown. Formerly not a Best Western, so not entirely plastic. Moderate.

Friendship Inn (306 W. Franklin St. 301/539-0227) Certainly no beauty, but cheap as hell, and a great location to boot. Local color element adds points. Inexpensive.

Harbor Court (550 Light St.; 301/234-0550) Great location, just across from Harborplace (demand a portside view!). Very helpful staff, with best concierge in town. Cute capuccino joint with scrumptious cakes in lobby. Expensive.

Hyatt Regency (300 Light St.; 301/528-1234) Typical supermodern Hyatt; lacking in charm but a good business choice. Expensive.

Lord Baltimore Clarion (20 W. Baltimore St.; 301/539-4800) Huge, cavernous, old-time hotel. Renovated, yet maintains the flavor of days-gone-by. Very central, too. High moderate.

Peabody Court (612 Cathedral St; 301/727-7101) Baltimore's grande dame, hands down. Old World decor, service, and style. Very civilized, if slightly stiff. A landmark eastern hotel. Very expensive.

RESTAURANTS_____

Bandaloops (1024 S. Charles St.) Another renovated townhouse affair, with good (yet unthrilling) food and yup-chic crowd.

Bertha's (734 S. Broadway) *The* place to dine in trendy Fells Point. Emphasis on seafood, but all is good here.

Brass Elephant (924 N. Charles St.) Perennial favorite, a classy Northern Italian joint. Elegantly restored townhouse setting. An expense account would help.

Conservatory (612 Cathedral St., in Peabody Court Hotel) Another old standby; very Bluebook Baltimore clientele. Classic French cuisine in beautiful setting. Staid, of course.

Dominique's (600 Water St.) Updated French; excellent, quasi-experimental menu. Younger crowd than previous two.

Great American Melting Pot (904 N. Charles St.) One of the city's latest; eclectic menu and crowd. (Light fare and finger foods rule.)

Hampton's (550 Light St., in Harbor Court Hotel) The restaurant on the tip of everyone's tongue. American fare, spotlight on fish and game, very innovatively prepared and served. Slight Southwest influence, but basically traditionalist—and very, very good. A must-splurge choice.

L'Auberge (505 S. Broadway) Arguably the Point's

classiest joint—classic French fare and more. And this neighborhood used to be funky!

Louie's The Bookstore Café (518 N. Charles St.) Fun, boho/artsy; a great place to hang out. Natural-leaning (but not overbearingly so) menu; great desserts. Do go.

Morning Edition (153 N. Patterson Park) Eclectic menu and clientele. Charming setting in Fells Point. Funksters galore!

Rio Lisboa (4700 Eastern St.) Every city needs a great Brazilian Restaurant (*cum* Portuguese fare), and Baltimore is no different. Very nicely done.

Sisson's (36 E. Cross St.) Trendy Cajun/Creole eatery that's informal yet very good. Local Baltimorean crowd.

Torremolinos (8 E. Preston St.) Unpretentious and very good Spanish place; fun staff.

SHOPPING

Laudable as it is as a hallmark of urban planning, the ultratouristy Harborplace really won't tempt you with anything to buy. The theme and design are middlebrow (at best), and merchandise reflects this stance. There's pretty much of an equal balance of ghastly tourist doodads, and those that are not quite odd enough to be kitsch; though, if you've always lusted after an oversized "I Love Baltimore" pencil with tassel eraser, don't let me stand in your way. Else, it's the usual collection of national chains. One exception: the very well-stocked cooking bookshop with quick-to-make dates staff. Oooh!

If, however, you're "lookin' for soul food and a place to eat" (that's Lou Reed, circa '73 to you babies), Harborplace is it. A definite step above most mall food courts, it's especially strong in the seafood department—at $4.50 a pop, I had more than a few crab-cake sandwiches here. Also, don't miss the "Original Maryland barbecue" stand (the pork's the best!). Oh yeah, you can also get salads, oatbran muffins, and other healthy stuff—but why bother? You only live once.

Charles Street is the city's main shopping drag, though anyone living in a larger city won't be bowled over by the fashions here. (Most of Baltimore's wealth is in the suburbs, and even suburbanites shop in Washington's more upscale shops and malls.) Still, it makes a pretty jaunt on a nice day.

Unlike D.C., Baltimore's downtown department stores have all been boarded up—a shame, since some are architecturally splendid. (There's nothing like an old-time department store.) The remaining shops on once-teeming Howard Street cater to a downscale, minority clientele, which is again indicative of urban flight.

Much has been made of Fells Point, but its shopping scene is no prize. There is a lot to hoot at in the old junk stores (I'd hardly call them thrifts), but there are virtually no new-clothing shops, and after three or four kitsch-stops, the scene becomes depressing rather than camp!

(For whatever reason, almost every store had a complete collection of framed posters of New Kids on the Block, probably garnered from an odd-lot sale.)

NIGHTLIFE

Baltimore ain't New York, but there are a couple of unexpectedly funky stars in its minigalaxy of nightlife novas.

Clubs

Ignore the hotel discos, yuppie hangouts all; instead, go to:

Cignel (10 E. Lafayette St.) Quasi-Bauhaus setting, house-and-progressive mix. Membership only, but no problem for out-of-towners to get in. Saturday, mainly—but not exclusively—gay. One of Baltimore's best!

Club Charles (1724 N. Charles St.) Best jukebox in town, great new music and more. A great place to hang, home to most of Baltimore's alternative crowd. Don't miss!

8 × 10 (10 E. Cross St.) Great place to see local bands, mix with a native crowd. Unpretentious, "fer sher." Much fun!

Hammerjack's (1101 S. Howard St.) Consumer warning: only for a heavy-metal crowd. Overstressed hair, passé punk jewelry rule. National bands sometimes, though, so don't write it off until you know who's playing.

Louie's The Bookstore Café (518 N. Charles St.) Listed under restaurants, but also a late-night pit stop. Classical/folk performers, often; '60s/boho atmosphere. But hey, it can be fun.

Max's On Broadway (735 S. Broadway) The best place to see nationally recognized bands, but more than slightly overpriced. That's capitalism for you.

The Depot (1728 N. Charles St.) Supertrendies, often superyoung, too. A bit much on weekends, when they are packed like sardines, but you should plan to stop by at least once while in town.

The Rev (1818 Maryland St.) More interesting for the innovative DJ than the crowd. 'Nuff said?

32nd Street Plaza (411 E. 32nd St.) is the city's premiere black dance spot, hosting a well-heeled, upscale clientele. Very nice jazz room, Rose Room for civilized conversation, and roaring disco, too.

Gay

Allegro (1101 Cathedral St.) Patently unfashionable music and crowd, but—they tell me—Baltimore's number two gay bar. Don't waste your time.

Atlantis (615 Fallsway St.) The closest Baltimore gets to sleaze—nude go-go boys on bar. Wow!

Hippo (1 W. Eager St.) A Baltimore institution since the beginning of time. Disco (*très* '70s) and more updated video bar. A handful of hipsters only, but the city's leading gay haunt.

BOSTON

Is there a boy or girl in America with a combined SAT score in four figures who did not spend the obligatory "looking-at-colleges" weekend in Beantown? (All right—if you're not from the Northeast, you're officially excused.)

Because that represented my first and only trip to Boston, I looked forward to a return visit with modest interest (if less than mounting excitement). It's not that there was anything in particular I wanted to do or see, but having failed to go to school in the definitive college town, I had to know what—if anything—I was missing.

For the fashion-obsessed young'un, the answer is: not much. Boston is a lovely city and, I'm sure, a perfectly nice place to live, but one gets the impression that it hasn't changed much in the last, say, 200 years. Bostonians pride themselves on their long history of intellectual rigor and social tolerance, but a mecca of trends, it ain't. Traditionalism in education is laudable (who wouldn't rather go to Harvard than Oshkosh State?), but in other areas—like leading a thrilling life—it is not. Going to nightspots filled with people in shetland sweaters doesn't exactly get me all fired up. As colonial cities go, I'll take Philadelphia over Beantown any day.

But don't despair: you may not want to live in Boston if the cutting edge is your thing, but that doesn't mean a short visit isn't worth your while. To my mind, the colonial architecture alone is worth the trip. Beacon Hill, especially, is one of the loveliest residential neighborhoods/historic districts in the country. So what if the residents OD slightly on L.L. Bean?

My favorite neighborhood is the northernmost part of the South End, an "in" area that has recently begun to explode with trendy restaurants and shops. The residents aren't exactly urban pioneers—it's both too close to Back Bay and too unslummy for that honor to be bestowed—but the presence of young professionals and gays has stirred new life, if not quite the burst of energy one feels in other urban cores. But the South End's Tremont Street is still a great place to explore by day (for the shops) or by night (for the burgeoning restaurant scene).

In terms of high culture, Boston stands at the top of the nation's list. It's particularly heartening to see the thriving theater scene, one of the liveliest and most vital in the country. The native, as well as student interest certainly help to foster it.

Though Boston is perhaps best avoided during its cold winters, it deserves to be seen any other time, when a long walk through town is de rigueur. As I said, the city may not thrill you for long periods of time, but it's a nice place to spend a getaway weekend or visit a friend.

IN TRANSIT

I admit it: for me, train rides have always been big fun. And for someone who spends far too much time getting to and from airports, the ease of traveling from city core to city core is a welcome prospect indeed.

If you, like me, live in striking distance of Boston by train, hopping an Amtrak makes strong sense—especially since most short flights are padded by extra hours on airport buses and runways. Personally, I'd much rather use this time to work, read, or sleep on a train. (There's also the lost art of taking in the scenery. I traveled back to New York on a wonderfully snowy day, and the view was like a print by Currier and Ives.)

Inexplicably underadvertised, yet highly recommended, is Amtrak's Club Car service, available on many routes. Providing extracomfortable seating, service reminiscent of first-class airlines', attentive stewards, complimentary newspapers, and other luxuries, it is a splendid way to go. Business travelers in the Northeast Corridor should not fail to consider this genteel alterna-

tive to flying,which allows an excellent working environment for executives on the move.

Kudos to Amtrak: they really have been working on
the railroad!

GETTING CENTERED

Compared to other sprawling metropolises, Boston
proper is a neat, compact little city, one which can
be easily covered on foot on a long afternoon. In
fact, starting your visit with a walking tour is the
perfect way to get a geographic and cultural feel of
the town.

The area called Downtown is actually adjacent to the
North End, and, from a tourist's point of view, not the
most central place to be. Rather, Back Bay is the de facto
focal point; as such, it's probably the best place to stay
(But I won't take exception to those who choose the
old-Boston feel of Beacon Hill.) Back Bay is convenient
to Cambridge and the newly cool South End as well.

There's not much more you need to know; Boston is
easily mastered in a day. And who's to quibble with that?

HOTELS

Boston Harbor Hotel (70 Rowe's Wharf; 617/439-
7000) In the novelty category. You get here by water
taxi directly from Logan Airport. I dunno; it sounds
too schleppy to me. So be advised. Expensive.

Charles Hotel (One Bennett, Cambridge; 617/864-1200) Modern inelegance more than set off by local artwork and individually created patchwork quilts, which everyone tries (unsuccessfully) to steal. A fine place to stay out Cambridge way. High moderate.

Copley Plaza (138 St. James Ave.; 617/267-5300) The press releases call it Boston's "*grande dame*," and so does everyone else. Recently restored to its former splendor; only convention crowds detract from Old World charm. Very expensive.

Copley Square (47 Huntington Ave; 617/536-9000) The low-grade businessperson's choice: central and relatively comfortable, if none too tony. The Café Budapest within is great for East Villagers in withdrawal from Eastern European food! Moderate.

John Jeffries House (14 Embankment Road; 617/367-1866) Charming in an unpretentious way; old mansion on Beacon Hill. Staying here will really get you in a "Boston" mood. High moderate.

Parker House (Tremont & School Streets; 617/ 227-8600) A strong contender: charming oldster that's been around since time began. (Ho Chi Minh ostensibly worked as a bellboy here.) Gorgeous decoration and ambience. Expensive.

Tremont House (275 Tremont St.; 617/426-1400) Originally an Elk's Lounge, this average hotel is convenient to the burgeoning South End scene. Anonymity is the calling card here. Moderate.

RESTAURANTS

Whichever way you cut it, Boston's still a conservative town. So you won't find the glittering restaurant scenes of Miami, L.A., or New York. But one can certainly eat well here.

Funkier places, with a student/postgrad crowd, tend to be found in Cambridge, especially around Harvard Square. Boston proper boasts any number of high-priced, "classic" restaurants, as well as a fresh new scene on Tremont Street (see entries below). But remember, compared to other cities, the restaurant action here is pretty subdued. That said:

Biba (272 Boylston St.) Innovative, eclectic menu, would-be funky decor. "In," but certainly not cheap.

Border Cafe (32 Church St.) Popular Mexican eatery near Harvard Square. Fits most student budgets. Part of a chain—and feels like one.

Casa Romero (30 Gloucester St.) A charming Mexican place, a fine choice for a good, authentic—and reasonable—meal.

Ciao Bella (240A Newbury St.) Ditto. But the name! (*Molto '70s, non è vero?*)

Davio's (269 Newbury St.) Expensive, semi-chic Italian eatery in the middle of town.

Ethiopian Red Sea (544 Tremont St.) Proclaimed "best ethnic restaurant" by *Boston Magazine*. Always popular, always much fun.

Grendel's Den (89 Winthrop St., Cambridge) Middle Eastern/European cuisine in relaxed, atrium-like atmosphere—tall ceilings and wood-burning fireplace upstairs for University boho types. Bar downstairs with great happy hour food spread!

Hammersley's (578 Tremont St.) An emergingly trendy eatery, with special emphasis on New England-ish fare. Nice.

Harvard Bookstore Café (190 Newbury St.) There's probably a place like this in every college town in the Northeast—newish bookstore/café with forgetful waitresses, overpriced "French" pastries, and "light" classical music—but to a New Yorker, it's an item of exotica. Salads and such.

Icarus (3 Appleton St.) Among the most innovatively designed restaurants in town. Basement locale, upscale fare. You should go.

Le Grand Café (651 Boylston St.) I fell in love with the tiny, glass-enclosed terrace looking out onto Boylston St.; a wonderfully soothing place for a solitary weekday breakfast. Best java in town!

Olive's (67 Main St., Charlestown) Eclectic, funky-yet-expensive star of formerly déclassé, now gentrified, Charlestown. But between the cost of getting there and eating, it can be a chore for those not on expense accounts.

On the Park (315 Shawmut Ave.) Another happening place in the South End. Adjacent, by the way to

Union Park, South Boston's loveliest street—worth a visit for the architecture alone.

Passim's (47 Palmer St.) A boho must-do in Cambridge Town. '60s-style café; Kafka and Kerouc abound. (At least in print and in spirit.) A fine old place to hang. Incidentally, Tracy Chapman started her career here—as well as on the streets of Harvard Square.

Poor House (907 Boylston St.) Diverse clientele, (very) unpretentious locale. A good basic eatery for people (like travel writers) of meager means.

St. Cloud (557 Tremont St.) Funky (for Boston) crowd in an old historical building. American/Continental trendy fare. Very "in."

29 Newbury (29 Newbury St.) Well-known café/restaurant on important shopping street. A fine place to rest one's weary bones for an hour or so.

SHOPPING

Boston's shopping scene reflects the conservatism of the populace; very little will make you go ga-ga here. But if the shopping bug bites, here's where to go:

Charles St. is the main thoroughfare of Beacon Hill, and boasts the usual suspects of cutesy bookstores, antique shops, and handmade sweater shops. Pretty, but a yawn.

Copley Place (100 Huntington St.) is a nicely designed

urban mall, featuring mostly pricey shops, though nothing hugely striking or special.

Filene's Basement was once a unique budget Eden; but since off-price retailing is now a national phenomenon, you can do your sartorial schlepping at home (if schlep you do).

Harvard Square has been around since time began, and probably always will. Teems with funky/boho shops, bookstores. (Think Berkeley here.) Tons of coffee shops—for rest stops!

Newbury St. is Back Bay's main shopping drag; the stuff here tends to be very mainstream and high priced. No real unusual boutiques, only nationally distributed stuff.

Tremont St., the major artery of the South End, is a newly emerging shopping street, the best place for demi-funky duds and avant-garde doodads. Hopefully, this will develop as a place for new designers to show their wares.

NIGHTLIFE

Clubs

Sad to say, Boston does not offer a plethora of cooler-than-thou nightspots. (Crewneck sweaters and postpunk ambience will never the twain meet.) But there's enough to keep you interested for a weekend or so. Specifically:

Avenue C (120 Boylston St.) Underground/student crowd in the middle of town.

Axis (9 Landsdowne St.) The third part of Boston's nightlife triumvirate. Best night: Tuesday's DV8 parties are a must; hard-core/trendy crowd.

Campus Man Ray (Central Square, Cambridge) Youngish, funky crowd with wild house mix. A fun, get-down place. (Some gay nights; call to find out.)

Cantares (15 Springfield St., Cambridge) A wonderfully tacky Spanish joint, where hipsters hoot and haw.

Channel (25 Necco St.) Industrial-chic concert hall where nationally known bands come to play. Check the schedule.

Citi (9 Landsdowne St.) Part of the same complex, but more suburban crowd. Sunday, it's gay.

Gallery (965 Massachusetts Ave.) Boston's premier black club, racially mixed on Sunday for marvy International sounds.

Hub Club (533 Washington St.) Three-level affair with disco, stage, and bar. Some trendsters, but mostly yups. Tuesday's International night boasts new European/Afro-Caribbean/Brazilian sounds. Thursday, it's a primarily black crowd.

Roxy (279 Tremont St.) B-list club in the South End. Only if you're in that part of town!

Venus De Milo (9 Landsdowne St.) Currently attracts the city's trendiest folks. Neo-kitsch attitude and decor. House music rules. (Wednesday, gay.)

Gay

Buddies (51 Stuart St.) Huge complex with disco, game room, bars. Another '70s throwback affair.

Chaps (25 Huntington St.) Retro/'70s scene, untrendy crowd. "Turn that beat around."

Club Café (209 Columbus St.) Restaurant/bars/cabaret. Not for modern boys.

1270 (1270 Boylston St.) Somewhat cooler crowd, usually better looking and better dressed.

CHICAGO

Chicago: the Windy City, "the city that works," the home of Al Capone. None is an epithet likely to turn on the hot, hip visitor.

So, big surprise—Chicago is oodles and oodles of fun. There's tons to do, tons to see, and enough to keep you busy for a very long time.

First and foremost, Chicago is a Great American City, second only to New York in scope and size. Yes, Los Angeles may have recently exceeded Chicago in terms of population—and in this case, at least, Chicago is no longer officially the Second City of the United States. (The Japanese super-scrapers in LA's downtown make just a slight dent in the history and authority of Chicago's label as

America's "biggest" city after NYC.) Stand at the corner of Michigan Avenue and the Chicago River, and you'll be practically bowled over by the grandeur and magnificence of the buildings that surround; from a 360-degree angle, you'll think you're in the center of the world.

Whether Chicago is a world-class city is still a matter of debate. The tourism department claims that it is, which isn't at all a bloated point of view. What it may lack in fashionable sensibility (though the city is certainly no major slouch here), it more than makes up for in culture, industry, commerce, and ethnicity. In many ways, Chicago mirrors the ethnic and commercial diversity of the United States even more than New York does.

And like most midwesterners, Chicagoans are friendly and eager to help. Not only will they go out of their way in this respect, they'll also spend hours talking about their city, with enormous civic pride. I dare you to visit Chicago and not make friends!

Many cities make this claim, but Chicago is absolutely a city of neighborhoods. In fact, there are about 75 different neighborhoods within the city's limits, defined as much by ethnicity as class. To understand Chicago, you should tour as many of these as possible—and here I suggest restaurants as focal points—but if you haven't the time, try to explore at least a few.

Chicago's famed South Side (big bad Leroy Brown is nowhere in evidence) is probably the first neighborhood to see, since in many ways it is emblematic of the sociology of the United States today. Hyde Park is a semi-exclusive enclave containing the University of Chicago, one of the foremost centers of education in the world, and its faculty and attendees. But a stone's throw away in any direction is the rest of the South Side, a black ghetto in various degrees of disrepair—most irredeemably so. Chicago is, in candor, a highly segregated city, and reflects the same sort of social imbalance that is prevalent throughout the United States.

For the trendy traveler, Chicago offers a plethora of places to see and be seen. Concentrated in the River North, Old Town, and Lincoln Park neighborhoods there are restaurants, clubs, bars, and —best of all—cafés that are as funky and avant as those in New York and L.A. (Great cafés are, to my mind, a key factor in making a city a traveler's dream, and there are more in Chicago than in any other city in the United States. When you're between stops, or just want a cool place to plop for a couple of hours in the afternoon, cafés are key; a complete list is included here.)

Cultural opportunities in Chicago are also vast. The Art Institute has one of the great collections in the world; the Symphony Orchestra is equally renowned, and theater in Chicago is probably second only to New York. Small theater groups are especially strong here.

Whatever you choose to do, one thing's for certain: you won't leave Chicago uncharmed. Second City or not, it is a metropolis of the very first rank.

GETTING CENTERED

Chicago is nothing if not huge. Unlike, say, Boston or Baltimore—each of which has a central district that can easily be covered by foot—the city sprawls out over a wide expanse. You can get around transport-free in downtown; but to get to the outlying areas of interest, you will need a bus, train, or cab.

The intersection of State and Madison streets is, for all intents and purposes, the city's core, and it is the point that divides all other streets into north, south, east, and west.

The famous Loop is the central area defined by the tracks of Chicago's elevated trains, that was at one time the basic downtown grid. (This area has expanded, however, to cover a greater, surrounding plane.) The Loop, shadowed by the ancient train structures, is grimy and gray, and seems never to get any sun. It's also pretty downscale, the elite businesses having moved to Michigan Avenue and beyond.

The North Side contains the Magnificent Mile shopping district, as well as the tony River North district, home to much that is trendy and hot. Also north of the Loop is the exclusive Gold Coast residential neighborhood, including superupscale Lakeshore Drive. Still farther north is Old Town, another fun commercial district, and Lincoln Park (ditto), home to gentrifying yuppies and gays.

This geography covers only the tip of the iceberg that is Chicago, but represents the neighborhoods about which most visitors will want to know. Those staying for a prolonged time period will probably want to venture out, and all of the places cited here are within this region's scope.

HOTELS

Allerton (701 N. Michigan Ave.; 312/440-1500) Old-time giant, sufficiently anonymous and certainly not luxe, but a good, central location for the money (and probably more atmosphere than the huge chains). Moderate.

Avenue Motel (1154 S. Michigan Ave.; 312/829-5000) No beauty, but serviceable, and in a big city, they don't come much cheaper than this. Inexpensive.

Blackstone Hotel (636 S. Michigan Ave.; 312/427-4300) Excellent Michigan Avenue address, in a slightly tarnished incarnation (yet therein lies the charm). And it's priced right, too. Moderate.

Drake (140 E. Walton Pl.; 312/787-2200) Renaissance palace that is the best-known address in town. Elegant and aristocratic grande dame that speaks to sophisticated days gone by. A tradition and much, much more. Very expensive.

Hotel Nikko (320 N. Dearborn; 312/744-1900) Ultra-modern Japanese tower with all the high-tech amenities you'd expect (and a great Niponese restaurant to boot). The polar opposite of the Drake, yet as polished in its own way. Very expensive.

Palmer House (17 E. Monroe; 312/726-7200) Another old standby, in Chicago since time began. Not as glittering as once, but a good Loop location, good restaurants, and quite reasonably priced. Moderate.

Raphael (201 E. Delaware; 312/943–5000) Exclusivity and taste at a chain's prices; really a find. The best bet in its none-too-high price range. High moderate.

RESTAURANTS

Alchemy Café (1835 W. North) "American folk cuisine" is the M.O. here, and it's a cross between homey and upscale. Seasonal cuisine, very stick-to-the-ribs, cum artsy clientele.

Angelina's Ristorante (3561 N. Broadway) Faux-elegant decor, pretty patrons, first-rate Italian fare. Homey and great.

Ann Sather (929 W. Belmont) Local institution, a funeral home turned Swedish restaurant. Cheap fare, mixed Belmont clientele.

Bento Restaurant (3367 N. Clark) Basic Japanese (tempura, terikyaki, and such), basic prices.

Berghoff's (17 W. Adams) Decidedly not trendy, yet very old-time Chicago; around since forever, this joint dishes out *zaftig* portions of traditional Japanese fare. A good place to dine alone in downtown; some lighter fare (like fish), too.

Big John's (2845 N. Broadway) A tiny marvel with the

best barbecue in town. Open late; perfect food after one beer too many (I promise!).

Blue Mountain Café (3517 N. Clark) No decor, but Jamaican food par excellence. Hearty and cheap.

Busy Bee (1546 N. Damen) *Haimische* (read: no decor) and cheap little Polish place that's a direct descendant—or perhaps precursor—of East Village haunts. When the mood strikes.

Café Ba-Ba-Reeba! (2024 N. Halsted) *Tapas* have hit Chicago, and here they are. Art-filled walls, well-heeled crowd; just what you'd expect.

Elbo Room (2871 N. Lincoln) Nouvelle cuisine in ultra-trendy triangular setting. Pre- and postmodern decor ('50s meets futuristic here). A must!

Hat Dance (325 W. Huron) Japanese-Mexican cuisine, to various degrees of edibility. Eclectic decor and quasi-trendy clientele.

Kingston Kitchen (3151 N. Broadway) Another Jamaican gem, this one open super-late. Tiny, cozy, primo food.

Muskie's (963 W. Belmont) Updated '50s diner with expected fare. Trendies galore; lots of hair gel required here.

Oo-La-La! (3335 N. Halsted) Fashion victims in force; very see-and-be-seen. And the Continental menu ain't bad at all. Among the top three.

Pasteur (4759 N. Sheridan) Very popular, and with

good reason: it's the best Vietnamese place in town. Everything is wonderful here.

Planet Café (3406 N. Damen) Another diner update, with just-all-right food and better than that clientele. Good for a solo stop.

Prairie (500 S. Dearborn) American Midwest (cum Native American) food, done nouvelle-style. High-class trendy, imaginative, and very, very good.

Rust Belt Café (2747 N. Lincoln Ave.) Postmodern industrial decor, esoteric fare. (You've never heard of any of these dishes, believe me.) Not cheap, but trendy and much fun.

Shaw's Crab House (21 E. Hubbard) Old-time fish house with whorehouse decor and tip-top fare. Very reasonable for the huge portions of seafood and more. Not trendy, but an institution nonetheless.

Spiaggia (980 N. Michigan Ave.) High-decor Italian eatery that is ultra-upscale, utltra-pricey, and ultra-good. Dress up, dears.

Star Top Café (2748 N. Lincoln) Zebra chairs, pastel walls, great music abounds in this trendier-than-thou eatery. Fish reigns here. Very of the moment.

The Blue Room/ Mirador (1400 N. Wells) Probably the trendiest place in town for upscale market; _très_ Nell's NY. Very groovy, very expensive, be-seen joint, open very late.

Urbus Orbis (1934 W. North) Supertrendy, a coffeehouse-plus (thus its inclusion here), and the most with-it joint in town. Long bar made of various artifacts is supposed to reflect the architectural (and sociological) development of the Western world. A statement, or what?

Vaudeville (3441 N. Sheffield) Basic little place, with fun French and Italian classics. Kind of cozy; a great choice in between a coffee shop and high-class.

CAFÉS

One of Chicago's nicest surprises is its preponderance of hip, European-style cafés, especially in River North and Lincoln Park. They're perfect for postsightseeing relaxation, letter-writing, people-meeting, and caffeine injecting. Very civilized, highly un-Midwestern—and altogether welcome!—touch. The best:

Café Aroma (1202 W. Webster) Brighter, cheerier than most, good selection of magazines.

Café Pavo (3523 N. Clark) Luscious pastries, great coffee, friendly staff; open till 1:30 A.M. on weekends. Cozy and casual; one of the best.

Caffé Pergolesi (3404 N. Halsted) Bohemian ambience and crowd, lackadaiscal service, Kafka and Proust abound. Need I say more?

Ennui Café (6981 N. Sheridan) The name says it all.

Service staff are slo-mo indeed. But worth stopping in if you're in Roger's Park.

Espial (948 W. Armitage) Poseurs galore; more fashion crazies than the other cafés listed here. Great couches in the main room. Do make yourself known here.

Java Jive (909 W. School) Basic, leave-me-alone coffee house that's open till 2:00 A.M. on weekends. Unstylish food, very stylish crowd.

No Exit Café-Gallery (6970 N. Glenwood) A boho plant bar, very '60s Greenwich Village. Where *have* all the flowers gone?

Scenes Coffee House and Dramatist Bookstore (3168 N. Clark) Really—that's what it's called. Hard-core bohemia, very posey, very basic food. Which means you should go.

Third Coast Café (888 N. Wabash) Somewhat Parisian ambience, student-y chic. But a fine place to lunch by oneself. (Other location: 1260 N. Dearborn)

SHOPPING

Chicago beckons with a surprisingly sophisticated—and certainly huge—retail mix. As should be expected in a Midwestern city, mainstream is the rule, yet avant fashions can be found. Here's the lowdown on what's where:

Avenue Atrium is the prestige mall address, and plays

home to Bloomingdale's, Henri Bendel, and other upscale shops in a rather lovely setting. Almost exclusively female-geared.

Halsted and Diversey Streets of Lakeview/River North offer the main selection of funky boutiques, catering to the area's artsy/gay populace. Also try upper Clark Street.

Magnificent Mile is Chicago's hallmark of the carriage trade, and covers North Michigan Avenue between Oak Street and the Chicago River. It's one of America's great shopping streets, though for the fashion victim, there's not terribly much to buy. Everything from Saks to international designers to national chains. Worth a stroll nonetheless.

Oak Street is an offshoot of Michigan Avenue, with a good number of tony boutiques, the most interesting of which is Gianni Versace's shop. Others are conventional indeed.

River North is the gallery district, centered around North Wells. A small assortment of other shops, too.

The Loop has seen better days; ensconced as it is by tracks of the el, the whole neighborhood seems (and is) dusty and gray. Two big department stores, Carson Pirie Scott and Marshall Field, remain; other shops cater to a lower-class clientele. State Street is the main drag, if you care.

Water Tower Place features Lord & Taylor, Marshall Field, and scads of other tenants in this modern, eight-story place. But beware: though it's one of America's best known urban malls, the tone is more touristy than upscale. A quick glance is all you'll need.

NIGHTLIFE

Clubs

Cairo (720 N. Wells) Well-coiffed yups, some fashionites, upscale club ambience (with a bent toward the modern). Sunday is euphemistically titled "alternative" (read: gay) night.

Circuits (4357 N. Cicero) Club kids, early '80s classic musical sounds. Young clientele with the right idea.

Club 2828 (2828 N. Broadway) Local, thus not supertrendy, but it's small (a plus in my book) and often has great international sounds. A fun nonscene.

Club Lower Links (954 W. Newport) Very B-52's: garage sale furniture, nondecor, beatnicky crowd. Poetry readings and such; music on Friday and Saturday nights. Oh-so-artsy!

Esoteria (2247 N. Lincoln) Black-clad clientele dances to one of best DJs in town. Sort of motorcycle/punk fetishist ambience—dated but fun.

Exit (1653 N. Wells) Another leather/bondage (read late '70s) motif, geared toward the suburban neometal type. You know?

It's A Secret (3259 N. Leavitt) Fun, suitably seedy neighborhood bar with about the best jukebox in town.

Max Tavern (2856 N. Racine) Another local bar with quasi-fashion victim crowd. Worth a look-see.

Medusa's (3257 N. Sheffield) Very young, very avant crowd. Great music, posing, more.

Neo (9235 N. Clark) Mondays, Tuesdays reign here; avoid weekend crowd. A Chicago classic, and still a great place to dance.

NRG (25 W. Hubbard) Danceteria-inspired, six-floor giant, tends toward the student-y, but high-energy European industrial sounds; much fun.

Sheffield's/School Street Cafe (3258 N. Sheffield) Friendly, nonposey café/bar, open late. Light fare, readings and such. Very San Francisco-boho.

Shelter (564 W. Fulton) Warehouse decor, great disaffected sounds. Avant clientele out for the night. Can be much fun.

Weeds (1555 N. Dayton) A great postpunk dive, poetry readings on Mondays. Unpretentious, to say the least.

Gay

Berlin (954 W. Belmont) One of the hippest gay clubs in the United States: kitschy, bitchy, and more!

Straights, too. Theme nights abound; *the* place to find modern boys. Lots and lots of fun.

Paris (1122 W. Montrose) Primo lesbian dancespot, home to modern girls indeed. Light food. Boys welcome, too.

Rage (5006 N. Clark) Huge place, eclectic clientele; a microcosm of gay Chicago itself. Busy, always.

Roscoe's (3354 N. Halsted) Always-crowded gay institution, with bars, dance floor, pool, and more. A good middle-of-the-road choice.

Sidetrack (3349 N. Halsted) Popular video bar, one of the busiest gay places in town.

DALLAS

Driving in from the airport, I remarked that everything in Dallas looked like it had been erected just minutes ago. "Hell, that ain't new," the driver snorted, "them buildings been there goin' on five years."

Welcome to Dallas. Though natives pride themselves on their city's sophistication—and it *is* an outpost of civilization in the American Southwest—Dallas isn't much of a city at all. Instead, it's a Texan's L.A., with an even ghostlier downtown and a seemingly endless stream of Mexican-styled strip malls that extends for miles and miles.

This isn't to say that you can't have a good time in Dallas, but you'd damn well better be going there to see a friend. Otherwise, you'll find the experience alienating to say the very least.

If you don't have a car, don't even think about coming here. Public transportation is dismal, and you won't be able to go farther than about four blocks from your hotel room by foot (especially in the city's insufferable summer heat). Ain't no way y'all be gettin' to them malls on foot!

Dallas is a wealthy city despite the oil downslide of several years back; its superhealthy economy derives from a diverse base in banking, aerospace, apparel, agriculture and more. Having developed financially, Dallas now seeks a cultural base, and its nationally applauded new Museum of Art is, in both form and content, of the first rank. Similarly, a spanking new Symphony Hall has among the best acoustics of any in the United States.

While the reigning style of Dallas seems to be that of out-of-control nouveau riche—the producers of the TV soap sure got that right—there is a bohemian segment as well. Granted, it's small, but it does exist. To find it, head straight to Deep Ellum's Elm Street. The boys and girls working in the shops here (about six) will be sure to tell you what's happening, and might even deem you a visiting celebrity of sorts. (They did me.) While Elm Street is more vibrant (slightly) at night, by day it feels like no-man's-land; sitting at Another Roadside Attraction, the kind of funky outdoor café where you expect to see the B-52's, I felt like I was at Bagdad Café—a million miles from nowhere. (Then again, even Melrose Avenue in L.A. feels that way sometimes!) There are also some fun clubs on this strip (see below), and I caught both

Marianne Faithfull and Edie Brickell's acts without getting crushed in a mob, something you'd be hard-pressed to do on either coast.

In the end, Dallas is more interesting for what it may become than for what it is now. At present, you won't be knocked out, but the museum practically makes it worth the trip; and the city's a haven for mall mavens from around the world.

IN TRANSIT

Dallas is American Airlines' global hub, and there's practically nowhere in the United States—and now, the world!—where they don't fly. And when American is among the choices, the frequent traveler just doesn't think of any other carrier: not only is American's on-time record the best of all major U.S. carriers, but also the ground and in-flight service is second to none, here and abroad.

American flies from Dallas to over 80 cities in the U.S. So you *can* get there from here!

Oprah says it, and I'll say it: American Airlines *is* something special in the air!

GETTING CENTERED

Don't even think about a small, accessible city core; instead, think of pockets of neighborhoods kilometers away from one another, best reached by super-highways. Like I said, you will definitely need a car.

With this in mind, let's try to keep things simple. First, think of "downtown" as the center area, for argument's sake. Just to the west is the "West End," a so-called historic district, of which the only interesting thing to see is the Sixth Floor Exhibit in the Texas School Book Depository, a memorial to JFK. You'll also find the Marketplace, a yuppie *cum* tourist brick mall that'll leave you cold.

To the north of downtown is the Arts District, which is home to the excellent Art Museum and Morton H. Meyerson Symphony Center.

North still of Arts is McKinney Avenue, a brick-lined street that forms a five-block area of shops, restaurants, and galleries. The crowd here is yuppie, not avant-garde.

The bohos/avants are in Deep Ellum, across a free-way directly to the east of downtown. This is where you'll find the famous Elm Street, previously mentioned. (By the way, the name "Deep Ellum" is a pho-neticization of how blacks pronounced "Elm," formerly the city's honky-tonk/jazz street.)

HOTELS

Aristocrat Hotel (1933 Main; 214/741-7700) Won-derful old hotel in the middle of downtown. Excellent restoration; the best reasonably priced place down-town. Moderate.

Crescent Court Hotel (400 Crescent Court; 214/871-3200) Designed by Philip Johnson, it's all rather hysteric, and ridiculously posh, just like the city itself. (Natives think it's to die for.) Very expensive.

Fairmont (1717 N. Akard; 214/720-2020) Reflects the nouveau riche modern elegance of the city itself; two towers with superluxe decor. Very expensive.

Hilton Dallas (1914 Commerce; 214/747-7000) Perhaps the best chain choice for those who want to stay downtown. Not luxe, but fine. High moderate.

Hyatt Regency (300 Reunion; 214/651-1234) It's the building you see, all glass-mirrored and such, in the opening credits of the TV show. One of the biggest and best Hyatt Regencies nationwide. Expensive.

Mansion on Turtle Creek (2821 Turtle Creek; 214/559-2100) Old manor house on expansive grounds, it's arguably the best-known address in town. Many celebs and such. More tasteful than you'd think. Very expensive.

Quality Inn Market Center (2015 N. Market; 214/741-7481) A good choice for budget-minded people who are visiting on business at the Dallas Mart. Not luxurious, but certainly adequate. Low moderate.

Stoneleigh Hotel (2927 Maple; 214/871-7111) Not right downtown, but a stylish old hotel that could be called atmospheric. It does have more character than some of the superexpensive ones. Moderate.

The Adolphus (1321 Commerce; 214/742–8200) A historical landmark unto itself, it's *the* old-money hotel in town, and most visiting dignitaries with taste stay here. Very expensive.

RESTAURANTS

Anita's Cantina (7324 Gaston, #319) Funky authentic Mexican eatery in the East Dallas barrio. Carnival atmosphere!

Another Roadside Attraction (2712 Elm) Funky little shack with several outdoor tables, cheap sandwiches, and such. Owner/waitress Jennifer is a trip!

Baby Routh (2708 Routh) Offshoot of Routh Street Café, it's very nouvelle, less stiff, and much less expensive than its predecessor. Very nice.

Barbea's (8949 Garland) A real joint, with the kind of local stick-to-the-ribs specialties you'd only dreamed about.

Blue Goose (2905 Greenville) A trendy restaurant; pretty, with eclectic cuisine and a yuppie/fashion crowd.

Brasserie Callaud (4544 McKinney) Too expensive to really be a brasserie, it's nonetheless one of the finest upscale French joints in town. Expense account, please!

Brazos (2100 Greenville) Stylish, yuppified Southwestern cuisine. Ignore the crowd and love the food.

Buffalo Club (2723 Elm) My favorite place in town: American with interesting (but not nutty!) new touches. Supertrendy Deep Ellum spot.

Cafe Athenée (5365 Spring Valley) is an "in" eatery with alternating cuisines, including many that are off the beaten path. Fun and very good.

Crescent City Café (2730 Commerce) About the nearest to funky this town's got; a truly pleasant place to while away an afternoon. Light, well-prepared fare.

Deep Ellum Café (2704 Elm) A favorite among the stylish, and should be a prime stop. It's more of a restaurant than a raffish café. Sunday brunch is tops.

Dickey's Barbecue (14885 Inwood) Supposedly the best restaurant for bbq in Texas. But beware: you'll get hooked on the stuff! Cheap as hell.

8.0 (2800 Routh) Very much see-and-be-seen, with primarily Continental fare. A trendy spot you should not miss.

Frank Tolbert Texas Chili Parlor (4544 McKinney) Touristy, but ostensibly the best chili in Texas, thus a local color must. *Real* cheap!

Mansion on Turtle Creek (in hotel of the same

name) French meets Tex-Mex in this very chic, very upscale haunt. A sociological experience in itself.

Mia's Pizza (3005 N. Beltline) Wonderful, slightly nouvelle Mexican fare. Tasty plus!

MoMo's (3312 Knox) Funky Italian restaurant with similar crowd in boho Deep Ellum nabe. Worth a visit.

Routh Street Café (3005 Routh) Probably #1 in town, should be your place for a splurge. Experimental American nouvelle cuisine, regionally based, in exceptionally well-designed setting. *Très cher*, but worth every cent.

Sam's Café (in Crescent Court) An expensive, fashionable place to see and be seen. Southwestern American cuisine.

Sfuzzi (2504 McKinney) Yuppie Italian hangout. Good food, if you can stand the crowd.

The French Room (in Adolphus Hotel) The city's best classic French cuisine, with Louis XVI decor. Expense accounters only need apply!

Theo's (111 S. Hall) Upscale Deep Ellum diner, with regional specialties like chicken-fried steak, and more. High cholesterol, but fun and worth the gas.

Wattel's (1923 McKinney) American with French twist; trendy, upscale dining spot. And the food is really quite good.

SHOPPING

Shopping is not a pursuit to be taken lightly in Dallas; in fact, it may be one of your major avenues of fun. One of the Visitors Bureau's press releases dubs Dallas "the third-largest American fashion center"(after New York and what—L.A.? San Francisco?). One thing is for sure: the concentration of wealth has resulted in an extravagance of commercial possibilities. They are:

Elm Street in Deep Ellum is home to the sartorial avant-garde; the shop Slix is king. A complete tour of the strip will take half an hour at best, but for those so inclined, it should be stop #1.

Highland Park Village is decidedly expensive and, they claim, "the oldest shopping center in North America" (heard that one before?). International designers, etc.

Inwood Village (also called Lovers Lane, for the street that it's on) is a strip of high-priced shops that's less objectionable—at least it's outside!

Neiman Marcus' (Main and Ervay Streets) downtown branch is worth a visit; it's the only original city center store still standing. The king of department stores.

Northpark Center is a large, decidedly upscale, mall—if you're into that sort of thing.

The Crescent (200 Cedar Springs at Maple) contains

galleries, boutiques, and restaurants, and is teeming with new money shopping addicts.

The Galleria is Dallas' premier upscale shopping haunt, with over 185 stores including Marshall Field and Saks Fifth Avenue. Mall buffs will revel in the fun!

The Quadrangle is an outdoor center with upscale shops in a unique architectural setting. Less unctious than most.

NIGHTLIFE

Clubs

Art Bar (2803 Market) New space in Deep Ellum that seems ready to take off. Wear black or bust!

Bar of Soap (3615 Perry) Neighborhood laundromat coin pub w/occasional live music. Happy hour (suds?) from noon till 8:00 P.M.

Club A (5201 Matilda Greenville) Prime night: Sunday's trash disco (kind of like Susanne Bartsch's does in New York). All of the "A list" is here.

Club Clearview (2806 Elm) Underground heavy-metal crowd. Not for the effete.

Club Dada (2720 Elm) Boho stand-out; folk, rock, and more. Some nationally known bands. Unaffected and thus much fun.

8.0 (2800 Routh) Also listed in restaurants; fun place to hang for drinks and such.

Kempi's (in Kempinski Grand Hotel) Primo upscale (read: yuppie) hangout in town. Fashion victims need not apply.

Metronome (703 McKinney) A mixed bag: some hipsters, some yups. But on good nights it can swing. Open after-hours; the later, the better, of course. Worth a visit.

Prism (2600 Main) Fashion victims on parade. Which means you should go.

Rhythm Room (5627 Dyer) Top reggae spot for students, fashionites, and more. Worth a drop-in to see what's on.

Royal Rack (1906 Greenville) Reggae pool bar with quasi-cool crowd. At the least, the best on Greenville.

Strictly Tabu (4111 Como Alto) Top yuppie disco. 'Nuff said?

2826 (2826 Elm) Home to affluent North Dallas yups in heat. Only if you must!

Video Bar (2610 Elm) Hippest dance joint in town, home base for Dallas' avant-garde. A must-do!

Gay

Big Daddy's (3913 Cedar Springs) Pleasantly downscale, with druggy go-go boys.

John L's (2525 Wycliff) Upscale gay crowd, piano bar and such. An acquired taste.

Jr's (3923 Cedar Springs) Large video bar, crowded all night long. Everything from guppies to white trash.

IXTAPA

If I live to be a hundred (which, at the rate I'm going, isn't very likely), I'll never understand the fascination with resorts—at least for people under 50. When I have a few days free, I head for Paris or Philly or even Peoria; baking in the sun has never much held my interest, and probably never will.

But, since it's the kind of thing that normal people like to do, I thought I'd explore a Mexican resort for this book. If the sun is your scene, Ixtapa may well be the place to go.

Why? First, unless you want to spend your vacations with fat Americans, avoid Cancun. This brainchild of the Mexican government was created solely to attract gringo tourists; and God knows, they come in droves. Not the interesting kind, either, but people who have no more imagination than to book a packaged tour. As you can imagine, because of its isolation, everything in this otherwise dirt-cheap country is price-inflated beyond belief.

I was unable to visit Acapulco, which in recent years has garnered mixed press from those in the know. In its favor, it is not merely a prefab tourist town. It is a city in its own right, yet the jetset abandoned Acapulco long ago for fresher spots. (There is talk, though, about Acapulco trying to reposition itself toward trendies, though if the Mexican Tourism Office can't send journalists like me, God knows how they hope to achieve this goal.) I've heard more than a few horror stories about ripoffs, violence, and more. As a final note, I should add that Acapulco apparently has a fairly large gay scene, and thus may hold special interest for this market.

Back to Ixtapa. It, too, is a planned resort, with all the usual international hotel chain suspects; yet it boasts a charming sister town, Zihuatanejo, that affords a boost of local color and native fun. I am assured by those in the know that Ixtapa attracts more upper-crust Mexican vacationers than the other resorts, another feather in its cap, which also helps keep prices in line. Like other cities in Mexico, food and entertainment can be had for a song.

You have one of two choices when visiting this resort: to stay in an ultramodern, all-service hotel in Ixtapa, or spend a mere fraction of what you'd pay there and get a room in Zihuatanejo (or "Zihau" as it's abbreviated by the natives). The latter, advised for hardier souls, is *très* Hemingway, and certainly the more atmospheric of the two. Should you elect the cushier choice, don't go half-way; stay at the Westin Camino Real, *the* hotel in Ixtapa, and one of the most magnificent properties in the world. The design alone (can I call it Mexican-minimalist?) is outstanding, and worth a visit for anyone interested in design.

While Zihau has changed markedly since Ixtapa was born—think of L.A.-type malls and chain restaurants here—the village charm has not diminished. Originally a fishing center, Zihau is still a typical Mexican pueblo, and boasts enough restaurants and nightlife to keep you interested during your stay. (If you're the type who is not happy unless you're in a different club each night, Acapulco's the better place for you.)

And what more can I say? The bottom line is that you'll come for the sun, and everything else is just icing on the cake.

IN TRANSIT

Snob that I am, when I found out that Mexicana has only one class of service (due to the configuration of their planes; a VIP class will start with the imminent inauguration of a new fleet), I was prepared for the worst. Big surprise: the level of service can compete with any business class in the world. And not one member of the flight crew I met was anything less than charming.

You can fly to Ixtapa/Zihuatanejo via Mexico City from the following cities in the U.S.: Baltimore/Washington, Chicago, Dallas, Denver, Los Angeles, Miami, New York, Philadelphia, San Antonio, San Francisco, San Jose, Seattle, and Tampa.

GETTING CENTERED

Ixtapa is a string of hotels, nothing more. And the town of Zihau is about twenty square blocks, so there's not much to discuss here. After an hour's walk, you'll know the town as well as anyone who's lived there for years!

HOTELS

Hotel Playa Linda (Paseo del Palmar; 734/43381) Just about the only inexpensive hotel in Ixtapa, with more local flavor than the big chains. No beauty, but more than acceptable. Low moderate.

Hotel Raultres Marias (Calle Noria 4; 743/42191) A rather pleasant old hotel a bit removed from the madding crowd. Ask for a balcony room. Inexpensive.

Hotel Susy (Juan Alvarez 3; 743/42339) Small and simple, yet clean and comfortable. Inexpensive.

Posada Citlali (Vicente Guerrero 3, 743/42043) A cute little place where only Mexicans stay. Inexpensive.

Westin Camino Real (800/228–3000) One of the grand resort hotels of the world. Inspired architecture and design, four pools, private beach, gorgeous rooms with huge, sensuous balconies. Gorgeous! Expensive.

RESTAURANTS

Carlos 'n Charlie's (Next to Posada Real Hotel) Locals (some) and tourists (many); a popular chain. Small disco, too (you tell me).

Don Quijote (Los Arcos Center) Good Spanish/Mexican restaurant; the paella is tops. But those pesky mariachis; ¡*caramba*!

El Sombrero (Los Patios Center) Continental cuisine, pretty surroundings. Touristy crowd.

Las Escolleras (Boulevard Ixtapa) Scenic restaurant on the bay (*escollera* means jetty); Continental/seafood fare.

Le Montmartre (Galerias Ixtapa) French cuisine, to varying results. As you can imagine.

Los Mandiles (Near Galerias Ixtapa) Quasi-authentic Mexican restaurant, some locals. Fun and informal.

Villa de la Selva (Paseo de la Roca) One of the better places, it's a private-home-turned-restaurant, with good Continental food and a better view.

Villa Sakura (Paseo, near hotels) Lovely Japanese restaurant with nice Oriental garden and the expected fare. Can *you* live without sushi?

Christine (in Krystal hotel) Haut-disco, circa '78. The glitziest and most "in" place in town; no need to go elsewhere. Make reservations first.

Joy (Galerias Ixtapa) Young crowd, decent tunes, standard disco atmosphere.

Las Esferas (in Amino Real hotel) A hotel disco; you know the rest.

RESTAURANTS

Canaima (On beachfront embarcadero) The best place in town for superfresh, superdelicious seafood, for a song. Very authentic and fun.

Coconuts (Paseo Agustin Ramirez, 1) Zihau's top "in" spot, located in a wonderful old historic building. Seafood/Continental fare. Reserve a table in the very romantic garden if you can!

La Perla (Playa la Ropa) Seafood-based Mexican fare; informal atmosphere, wonderful food. Locals galore.

100% Natural (Catalina Gonzales) Frankly, I'd rather die than eat vegetarian, but if this is your bag, go munch the leaves. Mmmmm!

The Captain's Table (Nicolas Bravo 18) Steaks and

seafood, corny nautical decor. But always crowded (I wonder why).

SHOPPING

One doesn't buy fashions in a Mexican resort, unless one considers buying Ralph Lauren or Benetton abroad a charming custom. And the crafts in the tourist centers are overpriced; buy them on the street in Zihau. Still, when you get bored, you may want to wander into Ixtapa's shopping "district," which is actually a constantly unfolding module of California-style strip malls. They have cutsey names like Las Fuentes, Las Puertas, and Plaza Bugamvilias, and as they're all stuck together, it's impossible to tell when one begins and the other starts. (The entire complex has, maybe, 70 businesses, and is easily covered in a couple of hours.) There are some pleasant cafés in which to sit and enjoy an afternoon drink, though little merchandise of note.

NIGHTLIFE

Christine (in Krystal hotel) High-disco, circa '78. The glitziest and most "in" place in town; no need to go elsewhere. Make reservations first.

Joy (Galerias Ixtapa) Young crowd, decent tunes, standard disco atmosphere.

Las Esferas (in Camino Real hotel) A hotel disco; you know the rest.

LOS ANGELES

If Philadelphia is the American city most unjustly trashed, then Los Angeles is the one most rightly reviled. Nobody here reads the paper, knows how to dress, or has ever heard of Jean-Paul Sartre. And baby, this place could have inspired French existentialism all by itself.

I exaggerate slightly, of course—but not by much. L.A. is an eddy, sucking up even intelligent people and thrashing them out with only the ability to say "BMW, babes, and box office." Men and women of substance who move here have only two choices; they involuntarily allow their levels of awareness to drop or they leave. It was Truman Capote who predicted that we lose one I.Q. point each year we live in L.A.—and I'd say more.

Can you imagine the culture shock to an East Village boy like myself coming from the darkest place in the United States—everything, from clothes to decor, is black and going to the brightest, in less than a five-hour swoop. I haven't taken my sunglasses off once. So... welcome to L.A.

I'm not saying don't come here. But do make sure of this: either you've got a friend who will cart you around nonstop, or you rent a car. Die-hard urbanites who swear they can do without one, even for a few days, will go running to the nearest rent-a-car agency in seconds flat. Why else do you think people spend so much time in gyms here; they miss out on normal exercise like walking 20 city blocks or running to catch a cab.

I'm not saying you shouldn't live here either. The halfway intelligent man or woman can do less work than in Manhattan, make a tidy salary (especially if one works at a studio), and generally enjoy life. But if New York is a city whose crime, cost, and crud have gotten out of control, L.A.'s total lack of grit—besides the gridlock—can be a hard cross to bear.

In terms of restaurants, L.A. has a very happening scene, though it's the converse of San Francisco, where ethnic eateries abound, or of New York, with its upscale-trendy and bohemian fare. Shopping is world-class, as one would expect in a city where the almighty dollar is king. (When Europeans talk of the lack of spiritualism in America, no city is more emblematic of the label than L.A.) And the nightlife scene, while elusive, can be fun. (Call me superficial, but I get a kick out of slipping past wanna-bes to get into a club; things are slightly too egalitarian here.)

As you can see, nights are pretty well taken care of. But what does one do by day? The beach lover will have plenty to do; but those who enjoy weightier pleasures may be out of luck. Still, I would be unjudicious not to mention the burgeoning contemporary arts and diverse theatre scene. One can also smoke oneself into a nicotine frenzy at a hot new coffee house, which are detailed below.

In any case, I have just one final recommendation for you: bring a butt pillow or bust. You may not have much else to think about, but the driving equivalent of bed sores will weigh heavily on your behind.

GETTING CENTERED

Forgive me for laughing, but in Los Angeles, this subtitle provokes gales of mirth. In fact, the biggest indie EP in Southern California during the early '80s was the Plimsouls' excellent "A Million Miles Away" though the title actually refers to something else, it's a good indication of what you'll find in L.A.

Much has been written during the past decade about this city's lack of "downtown," and its creation of one in recent years. In truth, there has always been a "downtown L.A."; it's just that 95 percent of the locals have never been anywhere near the place. Downtown *is* the financial center, and a few new Japanese-built buildings have provided the veneer of an urban feel. There are even a couple of existing department stores, downtrodden as they may be. Still downtown L.A. just misses the feel that most thriving American cities possess.

It's too early to rule out downtown's renaissance, however. Businesses do seem to be moving in, if at less than hellfire paces (though they're severely hurt by the city's lack of available parking space—everyone drives to work), and a few intrepid artists continue trying to reclaim their lofts. Underground parties continue to pepper the map of downtown L.A. though they're attended by only a hard-core few, the fearless party crowd. And who could forget the venerable Al's Bar, which practically singlehandedly marked the re-emergence of L.A.'s downtown? Finally, downtown is home to the garment trade and abuts Little Tokyo and Chinatown, areas of touristic—and, to a lesser extent, outlaw party—interest. On the fringes lie poor Mexican communities, and on the edge of downtown, ramshackle taco stands.

Will you be an urban pioneer and stay downtown? Probably not, because even if you're politically correct, you'll still be isolated from everything of note. I would strongly advise making your base West Hollywood, which is probably the most central location to restaurants, shopping, and nightlife in town. (See the list of hotels below.)

You may find the beach a romantic option until you see where Venice, Marina del Rey, and Santa Monica are on the map. Los Angeles has a new wave of beach people (i.e., in-towners who carry "laid back" to a nauseating extreme by living 45 minutes outside of anywhere).

Both Venice and Santa Monica boast a restaurant renaissance, but the weeklong visitor will find both locations too far out of the way.

Describing the geography of L.A. could easily take up an entire book. No American city is as vast as L.A. You'll come nowhere near mastering its scope in one week. Instead, my advice is to take a deep breath, try not to get flustered, and concentrate only on where you need to go. In Los Angeles, no one is a master of his or her geographic fate.

HOTELS

Best Western Kent Inn (920 S. Figueroa; 213/626-8701) The cheapest acceptable hotel in downtown (if that's where you need to be). Inexpensive.

Beverly Hills Hotel (9641 Sunset Blvd.; 213/276-2251) No better address in town. Dates from the beginning of time (or at least Hollywood's); certainly not the trendiest, but nothing is more representative of old L.A. Recently renovated by an Arab. Bungalows are best. Very expensive.

Château Marmont (8221 Sunset Blvd.; 213/656-1010) Hollywood-style simulation of a real château, right off Sunset Boulevard, it's my favorite place in town. Campy as hell, former home to loads of stars; a creaky, kitschy old dinosaur that must never die. Expensive.

Checkers (535 S. Grand; 213/624-0000) If business brings you downtown, this is the place to stay. A boutique hotel along the lines of New York's Morgan's, though with an executive, not fashion, crowd. Wonderful service, and the restaurant (also called Checkers) is *the* place to dine downtown: California/Continental nouvelle to the max. Expensive.

Hotel Hollywood (5824 Sunset Blvd.; 213/462-5400) Clean, modern, yet uninspiring, hotel; probably the least expensive, safest place to stay in downtown Hollywood. (Real touristy, though.) Moderate.

Le Bel Age (1020 N. San Vicente; 213/854-1111) Excellent location right off Sunset Strip, glittering showbiz clientele. Faux-European ambience and decor, all rooms are suites. I stayed in Madonna's! Expensive.

L'Ermitage (9291 Burton Way; 213/278-3344) Old World style, though (as expected) overdecorated to a hellish degree. Hifelutin', but with an expense budget, who cares? In Beverly Hills. Very expensive.

Mondrian (8440 W. Sunset; 213/650-8999) *The* rock hangout; a must for the music crowd. Supermodern, rather characterless, suites in would-be Mondrian mode; but you go for the guests, and for the pool. A trip! Expensive.

RESTAURANTS

Alouette (7929 Santa Monica) A time-warp French restaurant that hasn't changed in thirty years. Great classic food at dirt-cheap prices, and the 50-year-old Connie Stevens acts are worth the price of an entrée. A kitschy old never-was joint.

Atlas Bar & Grill (3760 Wilshire) Very hot new hangout for a funky young crowd (and, to a lesser extent, wanna-be yups). Food's good, too. Don't miss.

Authentic Café (7605 Beverly) A new Southwestern that attracts a trendy crowd with its pizza and pasta (neither of which comes from the Southwest, *bien sûr*.)

Café Blanc (3706 Beverly) Many call this French-Japanese joint with fab minimalist decor their favorite place in town. Supertrendy, and deservedly so. A must-do!

Café Katsu (2117 Sawtelle) A less expensive sister restaurant of Katsu, yet the food and stark decor are every bit as good. Highly recommended.

Café Mambo (707 Heliotrope) Trendy little shack; Latin-inspired New Wave food cum local weird art. Best during the week for a late breakfast.

Campanile (624 S. La Brea) High-class New Wave, California/Mediterranean place run by former Spago chefs. The hottest ticket in town for upscale-trendo (and, yes, movie mogul) types.

Canter's (419 N. Fairfax) Not the best Jewish deli in L.A. (Roll n' Rye in Culver City is), but the obligatory social pitstop at 3 A.M. Rude waitresses, hyper-choles-terol cuisine, but . . . go, darlings, and enjoy.

Cha Cha Cha (656 N. Virgil) Supertrendy spot of a few years back, now slightly beleaguered by Vals; decent food in Latin/boho ambience. Try it early in the week, and late.

Chaya Brasserie (8741 Alden Dr.) Tony French-Japan-ese spot (I know—they're as common as flies) in Bev-erly Hills. Beautiful people and surroundings of the oh-so-posh kind; go only if someone else pays.

Chinois on Main (12709 Main St., Santa Monica) French-Japanese-Chinese-Californian institution run by Wolfgang Puck. Say hi to Jane Fonda and friends.

Citrus (6703 Melrose) Among Melrose's trendiest, the theme is Franco-Californian, and it succeeds. *Très* L.A.

City Restaurant (180 S. La Brea) The *ne plus ultra* of artsy hip: warehouse with eclectic international cui-sine. Recipes border on the odd, but very "in" indeed (though not *in*-expensive!).

Duke's (8909 Sunset Blvd.) New site of legendary run-down coffee shop; nowhere near as trashy as the original, but '60s rock 'n' roll burnouts remain. The quintessential California experience, man. (Rumored to move again; check address first.)

Gorky's Cafe (536 W. Eighth St. Downtown and 1716 N. Cahuenga, Hollywood) Boho cafeteria with all right food, poetry readings, and such. Open 24 hours a day.

Hugo's (8401 Santa Monica) *The* power breakfast place in West Hollywood, home to stars, wanna-bes, and yups alike. Weekend brunch is always a scene.

Indigo (8222 1/2 W. Third) California-eclectic menu, with (surprise!) huge portions and unpretentious staff. Perennially "in."

Katsu (1972 Hillhurst) New Wave minimalist sushi place, utterly first rate. Expensive, but try not to miss.

Le Chardonnay (8284 Melrose) Lovely French bistro, very Parisian, and thus a welcome respite from the Melrose trend scene.

L'Orangeria (903 N. La Brea) Arguably, the best *haute cuisine Française* in L.A. Ridiculously expensive, but if the company will pay, then go.

Louis XIV (606 N. La Brea) Cozy, provincial French place, traditional and fine. A wonderful spot for a date.

Matsuhisa (129 N. La Cienega) Some say it's the best sushi in L.A.—and that's saying quite a lot. Cooked seafood dishes, with a Peruvian flair, are also top of the line. No one who eats here isn't impressed.

Millie's (3524 Sunset Blvd.) Silverlake institution whose weekend breakfasts attract a pleasantly druggy, rock 'n' roll crowd. Wear shades and go.

Nozana (Ventura and Eureka in Studio City) Clairvoyant sushi chef doesn't let you pick; he chooses for you, and is always right. Amazing, and among the freshest sushi in town.

Rebecca's (2025 Pacific, Venice) New Wave Mexican on the beach, usually mobbed. But so very L.A. that it's worth the trip from anywhere in town.

72 Market Street (72 Market St.,) Very trendy Venice scene; nothing's more upscale—"in" right now. Excellent regional American fare, gorgeously prepared and served.

Silk (6721 Hollywood Blvd.) Offshoot of the marvelous Café Blanc, it has the same French-Japanese bent, but at a lesser price. Highly recommended indeed.

Spago (1114 Horn) Only if you must. This Wolfgang Puck shrine attracts mainly tired (or at least, nonhip) celebrities and middle-class gawkers who save all year to go—then get seated in Siberia anyway. Everything that's wrong with L.A. in one small space.

Trump's (8764 Melrose) California nouvelle with trendy art, food, and people. Definitely a scene.

Versailles (10319 Venice Blvd., Culver City; a La Cienega branch will open soon) One of L.A.'s few great, cheap, funky restaurants—the kind that abound in New York. Primo Cuban food at wallet-friendly prices, in typical Latin eatery ambience. Garlic lovers will rejoice!

CAFÉS

Highland Grounds (742 N. Highland) The most glittery new star in L.A.'s constellation of java joints. Poetry/psychodrama, annoyingly often.

Java Café (7286 Beverly) Classic coffeehouse, somewhat more yuppified than in earlier times, but still a fun place to hang. I saw Julia Roberts chain smoking here!

Onyx (1804 N. Vermont) *The* café in town, home to all the hippest boys and girls, from boho to fashion-afflicted to truly smart. (Some read books—gasp!) You could die waiting for a cappuccino—but this is California, alas.

Pik Me Up (5437 W. 6th St.) Café with stars, trendies, bohos, would-bes, and more. By now, an L.A. institution.

Rob Roy (2501 W. 6th St.) Where have all the flowers gone? Why, here, my dear, here. Suzanne Vega wanna-bes and fashion victims in equal amounts. Only retarded wait staff dims the fun.

The Living Room (2636 Crenshaw) New coffee bar

that looks to be hot. (Correct me if I'm wrong—please!)

SHOPPING

Clothes in L.A. are certainly as cool as those in New York, but the shopping environment isn't as inspiring as Paris' or Manhattan's, the fashion victim will still find much to buy. Here's where:

Beverly Center is *the* mall in a city that sometimes seems to be nothing more than one big mall; of the huge shopping centers, this is the one with the hippest stores. Don't overlook the multiplex cinema, which often has first run art/European films.

California Mart has once-a-month sales of designer clothes in their downtown facility; a schlep, but major savings can be had on great stuff, so worth it. Usually the first Friday of every month, but call to make sure.

Fred Segal is the Barney's of the West Coast, on a rather smaller scale. Designers from haut to avant-garde for women and men; superexpensive, but lustworthy indeed.

Melrose Avenue is by now world-famous for its avant-garde boutiques. The main drag runs between, say, La

Cienega and La Brea, and contains everything from super-high-priced shops to Korean-owned ear-piercing joints. Best avoided on weekend afternoons when the Valley set streams in.

Miracle Mile (Wilshire between Highland and Fairfax) is not as impressive as Chicago's, and caters mainly to the executive crowd: standard international boutiques and such.

Rodeo Drive (off Santa Monica) is a symbol unto itself of conspicuous consumption of the gaudiest kind. Rich, over-coiffed tourists and movie stars abound—with hefty doses of high-class hookers thrown in for good measure. Who else would buy a cream-colored suit from Bijan? Go and laugh. (hysterically).

Sunset Plaza (Sunset near Tower Records) reflects L.A. pretentiousness at its worst—avoid the overstressed hair at the cafés—but some of the shops have avant-garde and/or *recherché* European stuff. *Très cher*, though.

NIGHTLIFE

Clubs

Arena (6655 Santa Monica Blvd.) Gargantuan new venue providing a home for the too-cool crowd. Conspicuous VIP lounge lends a pleasantly nonegalitarian air. Happening now, but a place this big has numbered days.

Cat and Fiddle (6530 Sunset Blvd.) Darts and ale, quizzically (but authentic!) British decor. Great outside seating by day, funkola crowd by night. Must be seen to be believed.

Coronet Pub (La Cienega N. of Beverly) All-purpose disaffected bar: everything from bikers to metal types to slumming gays. And everything else in between. *Not* high-class.

Crush Bar (1743 Cahuenga) Motown/soul rules in this always-crowded space: too big for a bar, too small for a club, but perfect anyway. No air-conditioning, usually, so dress accordingly. Young-ish, modern crowd.

Dresden Room (Hillhurst) A remnant from the '40s, and kitsch for days: Vegas-inspired decor, show, and more. The "in" crowd tries to take this place over in fits and starts, but it's worth a major hoot regardless who's here.

5th Avenue (429 Santa Monica Blvd.) Upscale nightspot, filled with monied/industry/fashion types and those looking for them. (Aren't you?)

Ground Zero (Call 669-1000 for information) This hotline number provides the scoop on Zero and 1970, both run by the same cadre of club kids. (Note: the latter is almost always at 836 N. Highland.) Fashion-ready, X-ed out, young crowd.

King King (467 S. La Brea) Bad, loud musicians take the stage in this former Chinese cocktail lounge almost every night of the week. Open till 3 A.M., usually; the later you go, the better your chance of missing the band so that only the truly cool remain.

Mayan (1038 S. Hill) Theater-turned-dance-hall that looks to have claimed the downtown crowd who left Vertigo when it went yuppie-straight. Too early to tell, but should be a hit.

Moonshine Club (ask locals for address of the moment) A West L.A. institution, one of the more famous underground nights in town. (Friday usually, but who knows?) All the more worth finding because it takes some time. But its elusiveness means no fringe-y crowd.

Nectar Club (East of Alameda) A downtown institution, filled to the rafters with the crème of the club crowd. After-hours, usually; 2 A.M.'s the best time to go. And make sure you do.

2nd Coming (850 S. Bonnie Brae) Unbelievably cool, yet elusive as hell: the cops closed this one down twice in the space of two weeks. So will it be here when you are? Hard to tell, though it's certainly worth a try.

Shamrock (4600 Hollywood Blvd.) Live bands, mainly garage-y, and hard-core Hollywood crowd. Not for the faint of heart.

Tiki Ti (4427 Sunset Blvd.) Polynesian motif, funky

crowd, dizzying drinks. Where else could this happen but L.A.?

X-Poseur 54 (6655 Santa Monica Blvd.) Wednesday and Sunday at Circus Disco. The usual fashion-victim crowd, with a slant toward metal chic. Understood?

Gay

Catch One (4067 W. Pico) Heir apparent to late, great Paradise Garage in New York: a get-down, mainly black club that also attracts supertrendy straights (Madonna, for one, unless you think she and Sandra are still *ensemble*). Druggy to the max, and think twice about leaving a car worth more than five grand any-where near this place—the neighborhood's the pits.

Plaza (739 N. LaBrea) The most elaborate drag show in America, outdoing even that of New York's La Es-cualita. Utterly tacky, mainly Latin dance club that's the biggest hoot in town. A laugh-fest, for sure.

Sit and Spin (at the Plaza on Tuesday nights) Ostensibly the coolest gay club in town, it changes locations, but is usually held on Tuesday nights. Young, postpunk boys (and sometimes girls) dance to great house rock; shows (mainly haut-drag), most of the time.

Revolver/Mickey's/Rage (one block apart on the Santa Monica strip, near Larrabee) Models, actors, bleached blonds, horny industry queens, et al.—odi-ous to the max. Untrendy pretty boys go here.

MEXICO CITY

Is Mexico City the largest metropolis in the world? With over 18 million inhabitants, it would certainly seem so (yet if only 70 percent of Americans report to the census, God knows how they count heads here).

Does it seem that big? Not quite. Mexico City is like L.A. in that it is a huge, yet fairly uncitified expanse. And there is not much urban planning, so it's pretty much of a geographical free-for-all.

Given the prominence of the country's resorts, few travelers think of the capital as a tourist spot. Mexico City may not hold the allure of the truly great capitals of the world, but a three-day visit is certainly not a bad idea, unless you're asthmatic, of course, or have respiratory ailments of any kind. Given the city's altitude, the weather (especially in spring and fall) is actually very nice, but the air is fairly thin. Add to that the worst smog in the world, and on certain days you may not want to venture far from your hotel. (Contact lens wearers will definitely suffer.) The smog is worse than ever, by the way, during winter, due to some thermal inversion principle that I'm quite sure I don't understand.

More than anything, Mexico City reminds me of Athens: a smoggy, somewhat gray, architecturally dismal capital, where even the aristocratic districts look slightly dim. (Of course, the less-than-cutting-edge fashions have something to do with that.)

Mexico has a larger poor than middle class, with an even smaller ruling elite. While the country has enjoyed (theoretically) democratic status since its inception, it has failed to enter into the realm of developed lands. The recent ongoing devaluations of the peso seem to have stabilized, and one hopes that under the Salinas government, Mexico's economic fortunes will change.

You will notice that the schism between rich and poor affects the city's social life, much of which takes place in private homes and exclusive social clubs. And, since the majority of night spots cater to the well-to-do, nothing like a street presence is felt here. (The New York phenomenon of slumming it in hip-hop clubs on the Lower East Side would be an anomaly in Mexico.) Thus, with the exception of Freak (see listing below), nightlife tends to be faux-elegant and thus rather dull. The cultural scene is somewhat better, though again perhaps less rich than one would expect in a city of this size.

In sum, it would be disingenuous to think of this as a prime vacation spot on anyone's list. Yet anyone visiting one of the country's resorts would be ill-advised not to spend at least a couple of days in Mexico City to feel the pulse of our neighbor to the south.

IN TRANSIT

Mexicana ranks with the great airlines of the world, and you'll be delighted to find that the in-flight service is top-notch indeed. There is only one class (how egalitarian!) at present, and it is equal to business class on most international flights. (The airline does plan to start a VIP section when new planes are added sometime soon; check into it if this is your preference.)

From Mexico City, Mexicana flies to the following cities in the United States: Baltimore/Washington, Chicago, Dallas, Denver, Los Angeles, Miami, New York, Philadelphia, San Antonio, San Francisco, San Jose, Seattle, and Tampa.

GETTING CENTERED

The megalopolis of Mexico City is every bit as big, and probably less well-planned, than you'd expect from the most populous city in the world. Wisely, the powers that be refrain from scaring tourists with anything near a map of the city at large. Nor should you even try to familiarize yourself with the entire town; no matter how much of an insider you seek to be, this is strictly a Sisyphean task. (And, as taxis are unbelievably cheap, you'll hardly need to tinker with the subway or bus.)

That said, the main tourist areas are:

Chapultepec Park is one of the largest public parks in the world, and provides a needed respite to the city's concrete. It also houses the city's best-known museums, including the Museum of Natural History, the Museum of Modern Art, and—most impressive of all—the Museum of Anthropology.

Insurgente is the longest street in Mexico City, running from north to south. Insurgente Sur begins at the Reformas, and toward the Baja California intersection becomes a busy, fairly upscale commercial street, with good restaurants and decent shops. It's more than a stone's throw from the main tourist areas, however, so unless you're visiting a friend who can take you to one of the eateries or the afore-mentioned "high-class" clubs, don't feel guilty for making it down here.

Reforma is the broad, handsome boulevard that passes through most of the city, beginning in the old downtown part. Modeled after the Champs-Elysees, it is home to the usual suspects of bank buildings, airline offices, and cinemas, and it is certainly the most imposing thoroughfare of the capital.

The Old City, whose center is the Plaza de la

Constitución, and which is familiarly known as Zócalo. This is the historic district to the city's east, and you shouldn't miss taking a stroll here, notably to the Cathedral, National Palace, and Francisco Madero street, the core's main shopping street.

The Zona Dorado is heir apparent to the Zona Rosa. Also called Polanco, it is a chic residential area whose main streets (Presidente Musaryk and Horacio) contain upscale shops and restaurants, without the salt-of-the-earth element that now pervades the Zona Rosa.

The Zona Rosa, to the Reforma's south, has traditionally been known as the most sophisticated part of town. While its reputation has dimmed somewhat in recent years, it is still a must-see after dark, when throngs of Mexicans line the streets. Dining at one of the open-air restaurants, the best of which are listed below, is something no visitor should miss.

HOTELS

Camino Real (52.743.321.21) The most exclusive hotel in the city, home to kings, queens, and celebs galore. A Westin property, it boasts large, well-appointed rooms, fine restaurants, and a secluded (yet not far from the Zona Rosa) address. Very expensive.

Caza Gonzales (Rio Sena 69; 514-3302) Actually two grand old homes with individually appointed rooms that are lovely and well-kept. Fairly central, and for the price, a true find. Inexpensive.

Hotel Edison (Edison 106; 566-0933) The place to choose in the old city ("downtown"), with a center courtyard and rather nice rooms; certainly it's in the middle of the historic district, which may be atmospheric enough to warrant this as a choice. Inexpensive.

Hotel Geneve (Londres 130; 211-0071) Distinct Old World charm, with modern-update rooms. It's central, comfortable, and thus recommended. Moderate.

Hotel Mallorca (Serapio Rendon 119; 566-4833) A very pleasant and modern place near the Jardin del Arte—not supercentral, but close enough, and you get quite a lot for the bucks you pay. Moderate.

Krystal Zona Rosa (Liverpool 155; 211-0092) This is about the best moderately priced hotel in the Zona Rosa, with amenities that belie the price. It's your best bet in this happening part of town. Moderate.

Stella Maris (Sullivan 69; 566-6088) Pleasant, very modern, and central enough; the price can't be beat. A good choice if the others listed are booked. Inexpensive.

RESTAURANTS

Alfredo's (in arcade between Londres and Hamburgo, near Genova) One of the best places in the Zona Rosa; classic Italian fare, very well done.

Azujelos (Camino Real Hotel) The Sunday buffet is a must, a very "in" place for upscale locals to meet and spend the afternoon. Ignore the mariachi band and enjoy the sumptuous and delicious food.

Benkay (in Nikko Hotel) The top Japanese restaurant in Mexico City, not to be missed for those in need of an (expensive) sushi fix.

Café de Paris (Campos Eliseos 164) The top French eatery in town; the crème de la crème of Mexico City eats here. And so should you.

Dos Puertas (Pedro Luis de Ogazon 102) In the ritzy Insurgentes Sur area, and favors a like crowd. Mexican/Continental fare, local art, charming decor.

Fonda el Refugio (Liverpool 166) A wonderful place for classic, delicious, Mexican fare with charming ambience. Touristy, but still worthwhile.

Fouquet de Paris (in Camino Real Hotel) Expensive, superluxurious French place, among the top three or four restaurants in town. Stuffy atmosphere, but excellent food.

King's Road (Alta Vista 43) Pub-type ambience, Continental food, well-heeled clientele. Not Mexican, but hot nonetheless.

La Mansion (Hamburgo 77) A marvelous Argentine place, a haven for lovers of grilled meats. Not trendy, but a wonderful spot to eat.

Les Célébrités (In Nikko Hotel) *Très* elegant French restaurant in international Japanese hotel. Business/expense accounts may best appreciate steep prices here.

Los Comerciales (Insurgentes Sur 2383) It means advertising in Spanish, and the posters, product samples, etc. that cover the walls bear this out. Always crowded; slightly gimmicky, but good food and top local clientele.

Passy (Amberes 10) French/Continental cuisine in one of the nicest settings in the Zona Rosa. The enclosed garden is a must. Not superexpensive for the ambience.

San Angel Inn (Palmas 50) This is the one place every visitor must go, probably the best restaurant in Mexico City. The excellent food ranges from Mexican to Continental, and the setting is a lovely, restored house. Your #1 splurge. Make reservations first.

Villa Reforma (Paseo de la Reforma 2210) The power breakfast place, but especially nice at dinner. Upscale locals abound; varied cuisine.

Finally, no visit would be complete without a quick lunch in the ubiquitous Sanborn's or VIP'S, the Mexican interpretations of American coffee shops. They're reasonable places for a cheap, and undistinguished meal; know that the Mexican food outshines the *hamburgesas* by a mile.

SHOPPING

As I mentioned before, the shopping scene in Mexico City is less than thrilling, with practically no indigenous design trade. The ruling class tends to shop in international designer boutiques (or buys their clothes in the United States), and local duds are tacky at best.

With this in mind, the most elegant shops are on the Avenidas Horacio and Presidente Musaryk in the Zona Dorado, and, to a lesser extent, in the Zona Rosa, though, again, I repeat that you probably won't find anything you will want to buy. One caveat: shoes licensed by major European names for manufacture in Mexico (Gucci, Botticelli, Charles Jourdan) are a steal; even if the quality is not up to Continental standards, you'll get a great-looking pair of classics for a song. The Zona Rosa is the place to go here.

Finally, if you want a dose of local color, shopaholics should head to the Perisur shopping center at the southern tip of the city. A cab will cost you about $6 for a 35-minute ride, and if shopping at Sear's (the major anchor) and observing local shopping habits is your bag, this is where to do it.

NIGHTLIFE

Clubs

Mexico City is not a nightcrawler's dream. There's really only one fun place (Freak, below); the rest are the playgrounds of scions on the local famous and rich. With that said, your options are:

Cero Cero (in Camino Real Hotel) If you're staying here, it's worth a stop; young locals and tourists alike, with an interesting, and de facto outdated, design.

Danzu Among the top local places, slightly more modern and less stuffy than most.

Freak (Avenida Universidad near Copilco) The only really funky place in town, emulating New York's East Village or London's ambience. It's about 30 minutes from downtown, so be prepared for a drive—and wear black, of course. Top choice in town.

Magic Circus (Rodolfo Gaona 3) Slants very young, though students of youth culture may want to stop in to note the local "trends."

News (San Jeronimo 252) Certainly the best of the mainstream discos, and the upscale young patrons (sometimes) do a good job of carrying off avant-garde trends. The music is the best in town, and the crowd the prettiest. Not a bad time at all.

Gay

Disco 9 (Londres 156 Mezanine) A hotspot of long standing. Very "disco" indeed. Turn the beat around!

El Taller (Florencia 37a) A crowded, smoky disco, one of the more popular in town, with fun American sounds and cute boys.

MIAMI BEACH

Listen up and listen good. Miami's South Beach/Art Deco area is hip as hell and is getting hotter all the time.

In fact, after New York, San Francisco, and L.A., there is no more happening place in the United States. South Beach boasts more trendies per square inch than any other zone in the fifty states—with the exception of Manhattan's East Village of course.

Yes, the blue-haired ladies are still here, though they—and the highly dreaded middle-class tourists from New York—tend to frequent North Miami Beach. Still, the *muy* chic Ocean Avenue area has not been overdeveloped, and friendly retirees live in harmony with (and are slightly awestruck by) the recently descended trendy trade.

Best of all is the definite European presence, which tends to grow stronger by the day. The Continental fashion mags actually picked up on the SoBe renaissance before ours did, and at too-cool restaurants, one always hears French and German being flung around the room.

By any standard, the South Beach restaurant scene is happening indeed. On any night, it recalls the frenzy of Parisian café society, with table-hopping and kissing the norm. To some extent,this reflects the Latin influence; its unguarded romance is the perfect antidote to Manhattan's innate coldness.

The influence of the Latin community—primarily Cuban here—is impossible to ignore. At last count, 60 percent of Miamians were of Hispanic heritage, and its Mayor Xavier Suarez was born in Cuba. The de facto minority status of Anglos presents an interesting socioeconomic situation: while some whites (especially those at the low end of the socioeconomic scale) resent the ubiquitous Latin cultural flavor, they benefit from the economic surge the Cubans have helped create.

Unfortunately, Cuban affluence has exacerbated tension between their community and the city's blacks, who feel that Miami's economic expansion has left them behind. On the other side of the coin, Cubans— many of whom have fled Castro's regime—espouse a strong work ethic and believe they've taken nothing but the opportunity to make the most of their lot. This tension, aggravated by recent allegations of police brutality, has resulted in several incidents of unrest in Overtown, the black ghetto just adjacent to downtown. (Interestingly, it is included in the tourism bureau's "Neighborhoods" brochure, though visiting journalists are dissuaded from treading Overtown soil.) The bottom line is that Overtown is a dangerous ghetto like any other, not a joyous latter-day Cotton Club, and thus should be avoided at all costs. If Miami is indeed "the city of the 21st century," as press releases blare, it will have a special obligation to address the social ills that all urban centers have to face.

One final note: although this chapter is devoted to Miami Beach, primarily the Art Deco district, there are other parts of Miami you may want to explore. (Coral Gables, the exclusive residential area, certainly merits an afternoon.) But with so much to do in SoBe, you may find it difficult to break away from the action for even that long!

GETTING CENTERED

Miami Beach is a seven-mile long island that can be mastered in about ten minutes flat. The South Beach/Art Deco district is the one you'll need to become familiar with; most of the action takes place on Ocean Avenue—the beachfront drag, as the name implies. Collins Avenue, which runs parallel, is the other main thoroughfare. The trendy area runs from about Biscayne Street to 20th Street, and is quite small indeed. You'll probably not go to the North Beach area, which includes the dinosaur hotels.

The entire South Beach district can be fairly well covered on foot, though some distances will certainly require cabs. And be warned: should your plans include visits to Coral Gables, Coconut Grove, or other areas in the vast Dade County metropolis, you'll absolutely need to rent a car. (A taxi ride from the Beach to downtown, a relatively short distance, will run 15 bucks.) If you plan to plant roots in the Beach, though, your feet and cabs will do just fine.

HOTELS

Alexander (5225 Collins Ave.; 305/865-6500) Miami Beach's most luxurious hotel—and thus, the most exclusive. Older, refined crowd (but if you're on expenses, why not?) Very expensive.

Bel Aire Hotel (6515 Collins Ave.; 305/866-6511) A nothing place, but cheap as hell. Only to be considered for extended stays. Inexpensive.

Cavalier (1320 Ocean Dr.; 305/531-6424) A fine medium-priced choice on the la-la strip. Models and stylists galore. Moderate.

Hotel Park Central (640 Ocean Ave.; 305/538-1611) Ocean Avenue's most happening and tony hotel; *the* place to stay on the strip. Trendy, rather international clientele. Expensive.

Hotel Place St. Michel (162 Alcazar Ave., Coral Gables; 305/444-1666) It's not in Miami Beach. But it's the place to stay in the Gables, with immense French charm; a smashing choice for non-beach lovers.

Waldorf Hotel (860 Ocean Dr.; 305/531-7684) Fine midpriced inn atop *très* chic Sempers Club. A nice scene. Moderate.

RESTAURANTS

Avalon (700 Ocean Ave.) Tropical Gothic, to say the least. Trendy, busy, seaside haunt.

Boulevard Hotel Café (740 Ocean Ave.) Another contender on prime strip. (Note: the beachfront cafés are pretty much interchangeable, featuring so-so food and great action/views. Exception: Lucky's—see below.)

Café Des Arts (918 Ocean Ave.) As above, with artsy intentions. Or so they say.

Clevelander (1020 Ocean Drive) One of best-designed Ocean Avenue hangouts, though plagued with Causeway (read: nonlocal) crowd.

Fairmont Gardens Lounge (1000 Collins Ave.) A great brunch choice, situated off the chaotic beachfront strip; also, a strong option for a romantic (as opposed to personally aggrandizing) date.

Joe's Stone Crab (227 Biscayne St.) The Beach's

longest wait, but worth it: everyone wants to suck them succulent claws. Not trendy, but a must-do anyway.

Lucky's (640 Ocean Ave.) An international hotspot, and rightly so. In gorgeous Park Central Hotel, it recalls the romance and mystery of days gone by. Suave crowd, world-class cuisine.

Mezzanotte (1200 Washington Ave.) Tops among funk-trendy crowds. Not cheap—but what price fashion?

News Café (800 Ocean Ave.) The Beach's hippest hangout. Sandwiches, eggs, models. *¿Que quiere más?*

Osteria del Teatro (432 41st St.) Quasi-trendy eatery with grade-A Northern Italian food. *Delizioso!*

Poodle Lounge (in Fontainbleau Hilton Hotel) A world-famous palace of kitsch. Gawking trendoids mix with the shuffleboard crowd. A hoot!

Puerto Sagua (700 Collins Ave.) A funky find: dirt-cheap Cuban fare in salt-of-the-earth (cum trendy) surroundings. Beware cucarachas, soup hairs, and such. (*Not* for the squeamish.)

S & S Sandwich Shop (1757 N.E. 2nd Ave.) Another hybrid of funk and junk: fashion victims rub elbows with blue-collar crowd. Waitresses' hairdos alone make this place worth a trip!

Strand (671 Washington) Arguably the hippest haunt in a very hip scene. Table-hopping galore; much fun!

And the food, very reasonable, is top-notch, too. *Not to be missed.*

Palace Bar & Grill (1200 Ocean Ave.) Very popular beachfront café with semi-gay clientele. (Regardless of your gender, the cute Cuban waiters will touch you at least five times per visit. *Te lo juro!*)

Thai Toni (890 Washington Ave.) New, fashionable Thai eatery that looks to be a success. (Thai is new to Miami; could you die?)

The Forge (432 41st St.) Not hip, but a fine, old established restaurant in Miami Beach. Take your parents to this one.

Toni's Sushi (1208 Washington Ave.) Every city has their chic Japanese joint, and this one is M.B.'s.

Tropics (1550 Collins Ave.) Large terrace, sometimes with jazz. Always lively, yet with questionable (i.e., Causeway) crowd.

Wolfie's (21st St. & Collins Ave.) The Golden Girls' Sophia mentions this place a lot on the air (kickbacks, I'm sure). Picturesque waitresses, colorful old-timers galore. But the tourist-inspired prices are a crime!

SHOPPING

Miami Beach is chock-full of used-clothing and antique emporia, but oddly lacking in stores with new goods. Of the latter, **BomBa** (1259 Washington) is the hands-down favorite, featuring both local young designers and nationally distributed brands. It should be your first stop. But don't overlook **Hero** (725 5th St.), especially for its wide selection of avant-garde silk-screened t-shirts. As for thrifts, don't miss the great vintage clothing shops on Espãnola Way. Other such outlets are **Last Tango in Paradise** (1214 Washington), **Heyday** (683 Washington)—don't overlook the world-class selection of hot pants!—and **Now & Then** (412 Española Way).

Women of all ages should not miss **Dauer's Bra Shop** (243 71st St.), which Tara Solomon, the Society Editor of *Miami Beach* magazine, claims is the only place in town to shop for intimate apparel. (Apparently, Mrs. Dauer accompanies shoppers into the try-on rooms to impart her expert judgment on fit and style. How nice.)

You should also try to hit the Lincoln Road Mall, which boasts close to 200 small shops—everything from thrifts to time-warp Latin beauty salons. The '50s architecture is a special treat.

Monied travelers may want to venture from the Beach area to inspect **Bal Harbour Shops** (9700 Collins Ave.), home to (yawn) the usual internationally known boutiques. Other centers are **Mayfair Mall** (Grand Ave. & Mary St. in Coconut Grove), and **Miracle Mile** (22nd St. between Douglas and Le Jeune Roads in Coral Gables). The latter is worth a trip—a very pleasant stroll in one of the nicest sections of town. (When you're in the Gables, don't fail to eat at Yucca, a Nouvelle Cuban restaurant that's one of the very best in Miami.)

NIGHTLIFE

Clubs

Avenue A (Changing addresses) A traveling club that plays host to M.B.'s coolest boys and girls. Ask at the Strand or Semper's to find out where it's happening, when.

Club Nu (245 72nd St.) Formerly fashionable, now attracting pretty much of a Causeway crowd. But worth checking out if you're bored with everything else.

Eclipse (71 & Sunny Isles) Premier after-hours haunt. As expected, a totally mixed bag.

5th Street (429 Lenox) New black club that looks to be a hit. Owner Natalie, formerly of the Strand, rules with a loving hand.

Island Club (701 Washington) Monday's Lost Souls night is the time to go. Else, avoid.

Mac's Club Deuce (14th between Collins Ave. & Washington) Eclectic after-hours, to say the least. At 5 A.M., it draws bikers, punkers, trendoids, and more. But everyone goes—and so should you.

Penrod's (10 Ocean Drive) Beach blanket bingo run amok! Bad hair, Causeway crowd. Some people go to hoot (it's up to you).

Reggae Rockers Café (216 Española Way) New establishment with very rude door personnel. And ten people inside. You tell me.

Semper's (9th and Ocean, downstairs of Waldorf Hotel) A total Nell's clone: period furniture, bad live performances, sardine-packed crowd. Best withstood early in the week. But it *is* very "in."

The Institute (Drexel & Lincoln Roads) A warehouse space entered via a crack in a wall. Most Saturdays, but things like this are always a crap shoot, so ask around first. If it's on, it's hot.

Torpedo (634 Collins Ave.) Burning list place to be; ostensibly gay, but all the trendettos are here. Wild, wicked fun.

Warsaw (1450 Collins Ave.) Primarily a gay club, but some straight hipsters, as well. Pornographic/perverted acts, like New York's Lady Hennessey Brown, so be warned. (Susanne Bartsch should never have let this broad loose on the world.)

Also, don't forget **Calle Ocho** (SW 8th St.), where ultratacky, Vegas-esque clubs recalling '60s Havana are de rigueur. If a crowd is going, don't fail to tag along. ¡*Que linda!*

Gay

Warsaw (1450 Collins Ave.) is *the* gay club. Decor is '70s, but the house music is very now. At 4 A.M., everyone—gay, straight, etc.—ends up here.

MONTREAL

They used to say that Montreal was the largest French-speaking city in the world after Paris. But since then Kinshasa's uncontrolled population growth has put that statistic to death. What is undeniable, though, is that Montreal is still a great place to become immersed in Gallic culture, at a fraction of the time and expense it would take to get to France.

Of course, you'll have to do without the Tuileries and the Pont Alexandre III. In fact, with the exception of the walls of Old Montreal, you'll pretty much have to forego visual treats; like most Canadian cities, Montreal is pretty much an architectural mess. Truthfully, the only indigenous architectural distinction of note is the presence of second-story stairs outside of houses, instead of inside, a feature designed to circumvent higher taxes levied for wider homes. Let's face it though—that alone ain't much.

But after you've resigned yourself to the city's non-descript physique, you can start enjoying its myriad charms: the people, culture, shops, and cafés. Montrealers have every bit as much style and *suaveté* as the French, plus one very exciting wild card: they're super, super nice. And that means you will almost certainly be treated to a wonderful time during your stay.

It's pretty amazing how the French Canadians have held onto the customs of their motherland after almost 400 years. Most notable, of course, is the *joie de vivre* and epicureanism that sets the Quebecois apart from the staunchly English country folk. The difference is not only in language but in lifestyle and this is one reason the separatist movement has lasted—albeit through ebbs and flows of strength—in Quebec.

To my mind, the best French tradition that has carried over to Montreal is that of the café, which is a focal point of social life here. But don't expect the uniform design and menu of those in Paree. The cafés of St.-Denis and St.-Laurent avenues are as varied as the city itself; from sumptuous pastry shops to hipper-than-thou postmodern haunts, there are many to choose from; in summer, especially, terraces spill onto these streets, forming a social scene all its own. (A complete list of *the* cafés is naturally included here.)

Style is everywhere, and it's very much reflected in

Montreal's restaurants and clubs. "We are like New Yorkers," my guide confided, "because we live in small apartments in town and spend our money on clothes and on going out to eat." No matter when you visit, even during the legendary frigid winters, there's always a social whirl.

While Montreal is two-thirds French, there's an English-speaking minority as well. And the schism is not only in culture, but also geography: the Anglos live mainly in the city's western half (that is, west of St.-Laurent), the Francos street's east. Similarly, the notion of a "bilingual Canada" is a demographer's dream; the francophones almost always speak English, yet the opposite doesn't hold true. The country's controversial French immersion program, in which schoolchildren learn the language from an early age, is met with widespread resentment from anglophones.

I'll not delve deeper into the bicultural question, especially since any current overview is bound to become obsolete. As a final word, let it be said that the French are adamant that their culture not be subsumed into the English majority, and the government tries to appease the Quebecois—generally, to the consternation of Canada as a whole.

For most Americans, the big country up north is, if not out of sight, then rather out of mind. In the case of very happening Montreal, however, it's a vacation destination well worth keeping on the tip of one's tongue.

IN TRANSIT

Montreal is just a stone's throw away from many parts of the United States, and there's no better way to go than on the national carrier, Air Canada. Flights are available from New York (La Guardia and Newark), Boston, Miami, Tampa, Chicago, Los Angeles, and San Francisco.

Air Canada sets a European level of service for North America;, and when they're among the options, why choose any other?

GETTING CENTERED

The area of interest in Montreal is actually rather small. Ste.-Catherine is the main east-west artery, and is also the city's lifeline, running from the English to French parts of town. (Interestingly enough, the majority of hotels are in the former half.)

St.-Laurent is the dividing line between the two camps, and is very much a street with an identity all its own. It's the center of contemporary fashion, and its cafés and restaurants reflect this point of view.

Just further east is St.-Denis, another very happening place. It's the seat of summer cafés, and boasts its own commercial activity as well. In addition, many of the funkier bars and clubs are here.

In fact, the center of Montreal is small enough that neighborhoods don't really have names; one speaks in terms of specific streets. Of course, that makes getting into the swing of things that much easier for you!

HOTELS

Bonaventure International (1 Place Bonaventure; 514/878-2332) Maintaining the standards of Hilton International, this is the preferred business address. The Japanese garden and year-round heated pool are bonuses here. Very expensive.

Chateau Camplain (1050 Lagauchetiere W.; 514/878-9000) One of the landmarks of the Canadian Pacific chain, and one of the most distinctive buildings in town. Another great business hotel. Very expensive.

Château Versailles (1659 Sherbrooke W.; 514/933-3611) My personal favorite: a European-style beauty with gorgeous rooms and charming service. Moderate.

De L'Institut (3535 St.-Denis; 514/873-4163) Part of the School of Tourism, thus student-run and friendly. A restaurant on the premises is a steal. Low moderate.

Lord Berri (1199 Berri; 514/845-9236) A good mid-range hotel in an excellent location, not far from St.-Denis. A good choice for the budget traveler who wants to stay in the French part of town.

Queen Elizabeth (900 Rene Lesveque W.; 514/861-3511) The grande dame of Montreal, recently renovated. Somewhat touristy, but will sometimes offer good rates. Expensive.

RESTAURANTS

Au Coin Berbere (73 Duluth East) Couscous, other Moroccan fare. A well-designed ethnic delight!

Bagels, Etc. (4320 St.-Laurent) Basic Eastern European deli; *zaftig* food at the right price. Away from the *glitz*.

Berlin (101 Fairmount West) Top outlet for German cuisine. Trendy, if you can believe that.

Better (4382 St.-Laurent) Reflects new trend for microbreweries on premises. Plus sausages and such.

Café Cherrier (3635 St.-Denis) A classic restaurant/bar, with lovely terrace in summer. Not the chicest but a tradition in itself.

Café Melies (3682 St.-Laurent) Leading boho/intellectual café, very down-to-earth. Sit-all-day. Attached to the Cinema Parallèle.

Café le Siecle (4434 St.-Laurent) New, avant eatery that promises to attract *the* crowd. Looks like a hit.

Citronlime (4469 St.-Denis) Nouvelle cuisine with Asian flair. Upscale-y crowd, well designed.

Citrus (5282 St.-Laurent) An ongoing trendster with varied menu on upper St.-Laurent.

Continental (4169 St.-Denis) Traditional bistro *Française cum très* happening crowd. Very good food!

Fonduementale (4325 St.-Denis) For anyone who missed making fondue in French 4. Inexpensive and fun.

Kilo (5206 St.-Laurent) New restaurant/café with striking postmodern decor. May be the next big thing.

L'Agora (4621 St.-Denis) Bistro/café with young, modern crowd.

Laloux (250 Pines East) French bistro with well-heeled crowd and classically wonderful food.

La Paryse (302 Ontario East) Cheap and somewhat trendy hamburger place.

Le Commensal (680 Ste.-Catherine W. and 2115 St.-Denis) Vegetarian food with likewise crowd. But more interestingly prepared than you'd think!

Le Crocodile (5440 Gatineau) Very busy at all times; eclectic, schizophrenic decor. After work, yups; later on, the trendier locals. And the food—classic *grillades* and such—is first-rate.

Le Poste Café (1366 Ontario East) Open from 7 P.M. to 7 A.M. Very popular after clubs close.

Le Sam (3715 St.-Laurent) Arguably the hippest French restaurant of the moment, upscale yet trendy.

L'Exception (1200 St.-Hubert) Hamburgers, light fare, all very good. If you're nearby.

L'Express (3927 St.-Denis) One of the street's original New Wave restaurants, it's lost some luster, but still very, very good and definitely worth a stop.

Lola's Paradise (3604 St.-Laurent) Eclectic, funky bar/restaurant that's definitely in the know.

Lux (5220 St.-Laurent) 24-hour "le drugstore" gone modern: restaurant, magazine shop, gadgets, and more. Not as trendy as before, but a must-see in Montreal.

Shed (3515 St.-Laurent) Hottest show in town; crowded with trendies and wanna-bes all night long. Hamburgers, light fare, and drinks.

Tout Feu Tout Flamme (400, St.-Laurier) Brick oven cuisine; warm and romantic place.

Tulipe Noire (2100 Stanley) Chic little café with world-class patisserie.

Witloof (3619 St.-Denis) Mussels and fries, as Belgian as the name.

SHOPPING

For the fashion-conscious, Montreal is a shopper's paradise.

First of all, don't miss the department stores on Ste.-Catherine. Unlike in the States, staff actually help you here. Of this ilk, La Baie (being French) is the most trendy, and probably the best place to look for clothing.

St.-Laurent and, to a lesser extent, St.-Denis, are the centers of the avant-garde, and should not be overlooked. For both men and women, the wares you find will be among the hippest off-the-rack in the world. In addition, you'll find some local talent that is unique to Montreal. Among the stars are Parachute, Scandale, Haarlem, and Culot on St.-Laurent; and Anthony Saks, Nicole Riski, and Carton (wonderfully modernistic objects d'art) on St.-Denis.

NIGHTLIFE

Bars

Blue Dog (3556 St.-Laurent) Classic fashion-victim bar, right on St.-Laurent.

Cocktail Lounge (3518 St.-Laurent) A classic St.-Laurent haunt; don't fail to stop in for a drink.

Harry's Bar (Cours Mont-Royal, 1444 Metcalfe) Half yuppie, half fashion-trendy hangout in new mall complex. Not a bad concept—for Montreal's freezing winters. Much is underground here.

Les Bobards (4328 St.-Laurent) Always-happening bar that's a good stop before the clubs.

Le Set (5301 St.-Laurent) Supertrendy early evening bar with very happening boys and girls. A must-do.

Whiskey Café (3 Bernard West) Funky little bar in English-speaking section. When you're there.

Zoo Bar (3556 St.-Laurent) Berlin-ish watering hole, popular early evenings on.

Clubs

Balattou (4372 St.-Laurent) Very "in," totally unpretentious, little place featuring best Brazilian beats. (Picks up on a Parisian trend, don'cha know?)

Belmont (4483 St.-Laurent) Very fashionable new bar, full of pretty boys and girls.

Business (3510 St.-Laurent) One of the city's original postpunk haunts, all dark and techy. Still plays about the best music in town; weeks better than weekends. A must on your tour.

DiSalvio (3519 St.-Laurent) New haunt on the street, worth a look-see.

Foufounes Electriques (87 Ste.-Catherine East) Classic young, postpunk crowd, tending toward the downscale.

L'Alcatraz (1279 St.-Hubert) Variable music and crowds; check with locals before heading there.

Lezard (Rachel et St.-Denis) Currently #1, home to the crowd of the late, great Poodle Club. Very avant and cool to the max.

Metropolis (59 Ste.-Catherine) Excellent Fritz Lang decor, but too big to attract an acceptable crowd. Worth a run-through for decor, if you're in the mood.

Gay

Jungle (Ste.-Catherine & Montcalm) #1 disco dance hall, a somewhat tired concept, but packin' in the pretty boys (and more, of course).

La California (52 Ste.-Elizabeth) Wonderfully cozy café on first floor, pool bar upstairs. A local institution, always genial and fun.

Lezard (listed above) attracts the trendiest modern gay crowd at all times.

NEW ORLEANS

New Orleans has absolutely nothing to do with the rest of the United States. For all of its unabashed hedonism and *joie de vivre*, it might as well be in Brazil.

There's certainly something very ironic about New Orleans' location in the middle of Bibleland. The weekend I was in town, the city played host to a convention of Southern Baptists, who intoned a collective "Have mercy!" in the face of a passing parade of Tara-clad TVs. (Tourists seemed to enjoy St. Ann's Deli, which I heartily recommended, run by two obese cross-dressers. John Waters, take note: Charmaine, who works the register, *is* the new Divine.)

A related word of warning: as opposed to New York,

where the drag queens are doped-out and docile, these girls are *mean*. Most of 'em hook, and knives are pulled regularly.

Luckily for the town elders, these babes generally stay a few blocks away from Bourbon Street, the main French Quarter strip. Unfortunately, tourists don't, and the massive hordes of tacky hinterlanders and the concommitant proliferation of souvenir stands come close to squelching the city's underlying charm.

Close, but no cigar. New Orleans is so distinctive that it would take far more than a few fat tourists to make it banal. But do take note: if at all possible, see the city during the week (when crowds are always thinner) and inquire beforehand to make sure no conventions are being held. (Middle Americans falling down drunk and dancing—badly—to local bands churning out atrocious versions of top-40 hits call to mind that line from "Auntie Mame": "Life's a banquet, honey, and most poor suckers go hungry.")

Of course, getting sloshed is not the exclusive domain of the tourist trade. New Orleansers are party critters of the first rank, and revelry is not reserved for Mardi Gras time alone. In the Vieux Carré (aka the French Quarter), beer and mixed drinks (especially daiquiris) are sold "to go," meaning you can buy booze in bars and at store-fronts, then proceed to march happily around town—or at least as far as the next bar.

I couldn't begin to keep up with all the boozin' going down. Happily, however, I was able to satisfy my gourmandial tendencies in force. No American city is better known for its regional cuisine (though, personally, if I never see Paul Prudhomme on another talk show, it'll be too soon), and the Cajun/Creole specialties—especially seafood, of course—are world-class. The best eateries are the down-home, unpretentious ones, though fancier restaurants also abound. (Traveler's advisory: stay away from anything on Bourbon Street, where almost all of the places are overpriced. By staying just a block off the beaten path—see restaurant listings below—you'll be well rewarded by the prices.)

While you'll want to spend most of your time soaking up the local color of the Vieux Carré, don't fail to see other parts of town. If you're only staying for a couple of days, the Charles Street trolley, which goes all the way out to Tulane University, is the perfect way to go.

Culturally speaking, there isn't a hell of a lot going on here; but that hifalutin' nonsense isn't where New Orleans is at. In fact, if I could give just one more piece of advice, it would be this: leave your intellect at home and come to New Orleans to enjoy the more visceral pleasures of bawd, bread, and booze. 'Coz whoopin' it up is what America's #1 party city (forgive me, Las Vegas) is really all about.

GETTING CENTERED

There's really not much to say. Every tourist should stay in the French Quarter, and will spend practically all of his or her time here, the exception being a well-spent afternoon on the trolley, viewing the Garden District.

The whole of the Vieux Carré is about 12 short city blocks by 8, with the center being Bourbon Street, and a two-minute map scan will tell you all you need to know. The compactness of New Orleans' tourist quarter and ease of travel are just some of the city's ample charms.

HOTELS

French Quarter Maisonettes (1130 Chartres; 504/524-9918) A nice private guesthouse, cheery and central. A fine choice. Low moderate.

Lafitte Guest House (1003 Bourbon; 504/581-2678) Here, I will verge from my usual path of recommending the most expensive place to stay in, by hook or crook; when in New Orleans, a period guest house is de rigueur, and this one is, by far, the best of the lot. Charming rooms, all decorated differently, wonderful breakfasts, and a terrific staff. Perfect! Moderate.

La Salle Hotel (1113 Canal; 504/523-5831) Basic little hotel, though not without its charms; in downtown. The best budget entry in New Orleans. Inexpensive.

Le Richelieu (1234 Chartres; 504/529-2942) A former mansion, converted into a wonderful old-time hotel. Slightly ragged, but that's part of the allure. Recommended. Moderate.

Pontchartrain (2031 St. Charles; 504/528-0581) A stone's throw from the Vieux Carré; if you're going upscale, this is the one to choose. Charming and luxurious, the VIP's choice. Expensive.

Provincial (1024 Chartres; 504/581-4995) Lovely old hotel in French Quarter, one of the best for the money in town. Moderate.

RESTAURANTS

Acme Oyster Bar (724 Iberville) Another great, old-time oyster bar; no pretensions, only top-of-the-line, ultrafresh seafood. Ummm!

Antoine's (713 St. Louis) Touristy as hell, but great old-New Orleans decor, and among the very best food in town. You really can't not eat here—legendary.

Bon Ton Café (401 Magazine) Unpretentious, inexpensive, and gastronomically, very, very good. Always very popular, so off-hours are recommended.

Felix's (739 Iberville) Top oyster bar with, of course, other fare as well. Very local, cheap as hell, and wonderful. Do go here!

Flagon's Wine Bar (322 Magazine) Yuppified, yet local, thus recommended. The after-work crowd, especially.

Galatoire's (209 Bourbon St.) Not as expensive as other restaurants that are as good; thus, a find. Creole specialties are musts.

La Pizza Kitchen (2808 Esplanade and 95 French Market Place) Trendy, young eateries with about the best pizza in town. Not a local specialty of course, but maybe that's why locals congregate here.

Mr B's (201 Royal) Very popular local hangout for years; not expensive and very, very good. Nouvelle interpretations of classic Cajun cuisine. Among the very best.

Port of Call (838 Esplanade) No tourists here, just hungry New Orleans folk who want the best hamburgers in town, maybe in the United States of America. Fun.

Ralph's Kacoo's (519 Toulouse) Another fine, unsophisticated, seafood restaurant, much-loved by locals.

Ratout's (221 Royal) Nouvelle French/cajun eatery, currently à la mode. Not cheap, but worth every last cent.

St. Ann's Deli (800 Dauphine) Aforementioned gem manned by two she-men. The ribs, at $4.75, are finger-lickers, and contain enough protein to feed a small country for a week.

CAFÉS

Café Brazil (2100 Frenchmen) L.A.-style space, with outdoor seating by day and performances (readings, workshops, etc.) by night. The coolest people in town hang here.

Café du Monde (800 Decatur) is, deservedly, a New Orleans institution: a huge old café that never closes.

Overlooking the French Market, it's a fine place to watch the passersby. A must-do!

SHOPPING

Face it: you don't come to New Orleans to shop, and the town is far from fashion forward. The best antique stores are on Magazine and Royal Streets, though both are tourist-priced; only for the upwardly mobile.

Canal Place is the main upscale urban complex, featuring Brooks Brothers, Saks Fifth Avenue, and their ilk (read: far from avant).

Decatur Street is the city's most interesting commercial street, all the way from Canal to the Esplanade. Toward Canal you'll find Bongo, the premier punk-fashion emporium, a French Connection outlet (a must-do!), and the now-ubiquitous Tower Records. Down near the Esplanade are some wonderful vintage clothing stores, including Fred and Ethel's, where you can find used clothing for a fraction of the price of similar boutiques in L.A. or New York. In fact, taking a stroll down the whole of Decatur should be tops on everyone's sightseeing list.

New Orleans Centre, anchored by Lord & Taylor and Macy's, is the premier suburban upscale mall, though only shopaholics will have any need to quit the city and see the all-too-standard wares here. (Postmodernish, white marble decor is pretty nice for a mall, though.)

Riverwalk (on Riverside between Canal and Poydras) is another central shopping complex, albeit one that's altogether too touristy for my taste.

The French Market can easily take up an entire afternoon: a massive, wonderful, open-air emporium with everything from clothes (used and new) to furniture to books to ?? Crowded but fun.

NIGHTLIFE

Clubs

Blue Crystal (1135 Decatur) Progressive music from speakers, local art on walls. Black leather and spiked hair are de rigueur. New Orleans' leading alternative night spot.

Café Brazil (2100 Frenchmen) At night, innovative performance artists, singers, and more; where the city's cool meet and greet.

Dream Palace (523 Frenchmen) Alternative/mixed clientele, surreal galactic mural on ceiling. Looks to be picking up; inquire locally.

House of Desire (622 Conti, 2nd floor) Young, postpunk crowd; house music rules at this very hip joint. Sunday is "Le Disco," '70s revival night.

Max (601 Tchoupitoulas). Live bands, usually heavy-metal in direction, at venue in newly hip warehouse district. Check schedule for info.

Theatre Marigny (616 Frenchmen) Not a dance club, obviously, but a place of note: alternative/experimental theater reigns. A good place to see/meet local funksters.

Tipatina's (501 Napoleon) Outside of French Quarter, with mixed bag of performers; everything from "nouvelle jazz" (their phrase,not mine) to reggae, live and taped.

Warehouse Café (636 Tchoupitoulas) Another hot house for live bands, with more catholic bookings than Max's: R&B, new music, and more.

Gay

Bourbon Pub (801 Bourbon St.) Most popular in town. Downstairs: video bar; upstairs: crowded dance club. Young'uns.

Café Lafitte in Exile (901 Bourbon St.) Dark, always crowded bar, older clientele, drunk queens hanging from balcony, hooting at passers-by. Oh, Scarlett!

Corner Pocket (940 St. Louis) Sleazy strippers, hustlers, and like clientele. Southern trash at its best.

Good Friends (740 Dauphine) "Upscale" (read: no hustlers) bar with more queens on balcony. Good A/C.

NEW YORK

As I write, my typewriter and I sit amid a sea of boxes. No stereo, no coffee, no phone: you see, my friends, after more than a decade in New York, tomorrow I move to L.A.

Let the circumstances of my transcontinental transplant remain unsung. And while I leave the world's most thrilling city with deep regrets, I know that I am leaving my best friend . . . and perhaps something of a foe as well.

The bottom line is this: New York is a mess. What's more, as a highly intensified microcosm of any urban center in the United States, the city's ongoing, unchecked demise portends poorly for our future standard of living.

Consider the following statistics. Over half the number of inner-city high school students do not earn diplomas. Since New York's manufacturing base is shrinking as well as its number of blue-collar jobs; and since these young people are woefully unprepared for even low-level office jobs in our high-tech age, it is inevitable that the majority will never become productive members of society. Just yesterday, I heard on the news that violent crimes committed by 10- to 12-year olds had risen from last year's numbers by over 300 percent!

When I was at Columbia in the late '70s, I laughed at out-of-towners' fear of New York crime. (After all, wasn't I the one hopping subways at 4:00 A.M.?) Now I beg their caution. In all candor, I sometimes feel terrified on the subway even during the day; and I resent the wrath of gangs of kids—they're everywhere now. Bumper-to-bumper L.A. traffic may not be much fun, but (freeway murders not withstanding) I'll take boredom over terror any day of the week.

You'll excuse me, dear readers, for this cathartic exercise in lieu of my usual introduction. But what could I tell you about the most-discussed city in the world that you don't already know? You *should* come here, maybe even *live* here, but in either case, do take care. New York, unfortunately, is no longer a safe place for those who abide by the letter of the law.

GETTING CENTERED_____

In the most sensical city in the world, one dominated by a grid (with the exception of the Village) and clearly delineated neighborhoods, any explanation would seem senseless. A two-minute glance at a map will do you more good than I could possibly do here.

One caveat: if you are going to a street downtown (that is, in the Village or TriBeCa), call the destination first and make sure you have the exact location. Most New York cabbies are foreign-born, and can't even find the Empire State Building. If you know, for instance, that Hubert Street is four blocks south of Canal, you're already ahead of the game.

On public transportation: since most buses run across major avenues and streets, they're easier to figure out (on the average) than poorly marked subways. But during the weekdays, they take forever; try underground transport if you can. Do, however, be careful. As mentioned above, the proliferation of crime is such that one can never be too cautious.

HOTELS_____

Century Paramount (235 W. 46th St.; 212/764-5500) Tourist-level hotel in the theater district; recommended for the price of its rooms. High moderate.

Empire (63rd St. and Broadway) One of the few reasonably priced, decent hotels in New York; very convenient to Lincoln Center and Upper West Side (but not downtown). No beauty, but a fine place to stay. High moderate.

Gorham (136 W. 55th St.; 212/245-1800) Arguably the crème de la crème of New York's reasonably priced, small old hotels. Thus, recommended. High moderate.

Morgan's (237 Madison Ave.; 212/686-0300) The original Rubell/Schrager hostelry, with high-contrast black/white decor, high-tech bathrooms, the works. Costly, but less so than the Royalton and—downtowners take note—closer to the East Village scene. Very expensive.

Palace International (429 Park Ave. So.; 212/523-4860) Undistinguished modern hotel most notable for good prices and close-to-downtown location. Not a bad choice, therefore. High moderate.

Paramount (235 W. 46th St.; 212/764-5500) In Schrager's very hip new hotel, dazzlingly "in." Rooms are tiny but very reasonably priced, making this your very top choice.

Sherry Netherland (781 Fifth Ave.; 212/355-2800) Outshines Ivana's Plaza by a mile; one of the United States' truly distinguished hotels. Glittering jetset clientele. Very expensive.

The Royalton (44 W. 44th St.; 212/730-1344) *The* cool hotel in New York, created by Ian Schrager and the late Steve Rubell. Haut-minimalist decor with postmodern touches; the lobby and main room bathrooms are worth the price of admission. International stylesetters and local gentry wouldn't stay anywhere else. Very expensive.

RESTAURANTS

Avenue A Sushi (105 Avenue A) Black-and-lacquer Japanese restaurant in the heart of the Lower East Side. When you're in the East Village and are dying for sushi, this is where you should go.

Benny's Burrito (93 Avenue A) San Francisco-style Mexican food, boho atmosphere included. Funky East Village crowd, very cheap (but great) food.

Café Luxembourg (200 W. 70th St.) My one bow to uptown; still the trendiest place on the Upper West Side. Which means . . .

Café Mogador (101 St. Marks Place) Make no bones: this is my favorite restaurant in New York. I know Morocco, and the food at this delightful place is as good as the best there. The North African decor is charming, and the local boho crowd always has a good time. Belly dancing on Wednesdays; reserve in advance!

Café Orlin (41 St. Marks Place) The best café in New York; crowded, European-style, with more-than-acceptable food and better than that pastries and java.

Dark, postpunky, and *the* haunt of those in the know. Fight for one of the four tiny outdoor tables on nice sunny days.

Chez Brigitte (77 Greenwich Ave.) Counter-space only, French bonne femme cuisine prepared by Brigitte herself. Tiny and utterly down-home (au français), it's the perfect place to dine alone.

Dojo (24 St. Marks Place) The cheapest non-Polish joint around, with excellent noodle stirs, neo-Japanese, and such. Another place that *everyone* goes.

E.A.T. (11 St. Marks Place) I'm not a fan, but vegetarians like the quasi-imaginative cuisine and minimalist decor.

El Teddy's (219 West Broadway) Formerly El Internacional, whose passing was much-rued, it's back, and in a big way. Spanish tapas, pretty crowd, and more.

Espace (9 East 16th St.) Chic little place (French-y) in the photography district. Worth a stop.

Everybody's (31 Second Avenue A) Doll heads, *Enquirer* headlines galore; the kitschiest restaurant in town. But the food's no joke: excellent classic French bistro fare. Probably the most expensive place in the neighborhood, but great fun, and worth every centime.

Flamingo East (219 Second Ave.) High-concept postmodern design, eclectic menu, *très* chic clientele. One of those places where one *must* be seen!

Florent (69 Gansevoort) Florent, I hereby grant landmark status to thee! The first spot in the West Village meat packing district, it's a neo-retro diner with slightly updated bistro cuisine. Still trendy after all these years; that a restaurant should remain this fun this long demands kudos. (Special note: No cabbies know where this is, so call ahead and get driving instructions first.)

Indochine (430 Lafayette St.) Trendiness endures at this NoHo classic: Vietnamese with a nouvelle twist. Not too expensive (though you'll leave hungry), and still one of the toniest places in New York.

Jerry's 103 (103 Second Ave.) We locals rued the demise of the former 24-hour deli-like 103; how many nights were we there at 5:00 A.M.? But this new postmodern bistro has great food, great people, and decent prices, so all is well. Very "in."

Katz's (205 E. Houston St.) The workers are Puerto Rican, not Jewish, and the crowd ranges from local boho to suburban types, but it's so old-time New York that no visit to the city would be complete without a corned beef (or bagel *mit schmear* to veggies) here.

L'Acajou (53 W. 19th St.) One of the original photo district (also called Flatiron, for the building) joints, it was never superpopular, and still isn't—but therein its charm. Only well-heeled locals go, and it's a wonderful place for a meal *à deux*.

La Caridad (2199 Broadway) The classic "comida China y Latina"; tacky little hole in the wall with supercheap, supergreasy, supergratifying food. A New York state of mind.

La Luncheonette (130 Tenth Ave.) West Side French bistro in dinerette setting. Very trendy and fun, but more than somewhat out of the way.

Life Café (343 East 10th St.) A perennial favorite on the north side of in-the-news Tompkins Square Park. Classic East Village boho cafe with a Mexican twist. But can the performers, baby!

Lucky Strike (59 Grand St.) Ultratrendy in an upscale-ish way, i.e., don't wear torn jeans. Not cheap, but what price fame? Say hi to Dianne Brill!

Ludlow Street Café (165 Ludlow St.) Peruvian food (usually), utterly Lower East Side crowd, and, many times, bands. Dangerous barrio location; trust me, and take a cab. (Down the street is El Sombrero, a marginally acceptable Mexican eatery; ditto, transportation advice.)

Lupe's East L.A. Kitchen (110 Avenue of the Americas) SoHo standard, though the food is cheaper and better in East L.A.

Man Ray (169 Eighth Ave.) New incarnation of this Chelsea gem, this time by Brian McNally, N.Y.'s restaurant king; too new to know, but it's bound to be exceedingly "in."

Montrachet (239 W. Broadway) Pricey, somewhat pretentious TriBeCa Frenchy, more popular among haut-yups than trendies, but still a very romantic place to eat.

M.K. (204 Fifth Ave.) The club ain't what it used to be, but the restaurant upstairs is still abuzz, and the fare (neo-French) still shines. Very contempo New York.

Odeon (145 West Broadway) The Odeon was almost synonomous with the downtown restaurant explosion; a decade later, the joint still roars. Gorgeous neo-Nouveau decor, pretty servers, prime bistro fare. A marvel of the modern world!

150 Wooster (150 Wooster St.) Only *the* place to be seen in New York; the newest star in restaurateur Brian McNally's gastronomic galaxy. International celebrities and local trendsetters in droves. Reserve aeons in advance.

Provence (38 Macdougal St.) The noise is deafening, the air-conditioning's always broken, but the food (French, 'natch) almost makes it all right. Slightly less trendy than in its heyday, but a staple on the downtown dining scene.

Rio Mar (79 Ninth Ave.) The standard for cheap Spanish fare. Local color galore.

Spain (113 W. 13th St.) Utterly nontrendy: a huge,

underdecorated room, close-set tables, and the best, cheapest Spanish food in town. One paella feeds an army, so share.

Sugar Reef (92 Second Ave.) Don't snicker, my trendy friends; I know the crowd, especially early, is very bridge and tunnel; yet where can you find Caribbean food this good, this cheap? Go late and avoid the rush. A psychedelic island fantasy.

Sylvia's (328 Lenox Ave.) The most famous restaurant in Harlem, though catching a cab home is a bitch. Top-notch soul food; worth the trip.

Tib~t Restaurant (Second Avenue between 5th and 6th St.) A new star in the local East Village gastro scene: like Chinese food, but more delicately spiced, and far less greasy. Inexpensive, ethnic, and great.

Tom's Restaurant (2880 Broadway) When I was at Columbia, I lived on the liver and onions ($2.65; guess what century that was). Anyway, it's the farthest thing from chic in the world, but if you're up in Morningside Heights, you should stop in; the waitresses are worth the detour. By the way, this is the "Tom's Diner" that inspired the Suzanne Vega song.

Trixie's (307 W. 47th St.) Once ultratrendy, the yups have found it, and many downtowners don't bother with the $7-each-way cab. Still and all, this funky little place is *the* place to go in the garment district.

Two Boots (37 Avenue A) Cajun/Italian: a dream,

right? Yes, and a great one too; the food here sings. Funky, spirited East Village joint that's become an institution in just two years. New take-out joint across the street, too.

Veselka Coffee Shop (144 Second Ave.) The type of classic counter joint (think Edward Hopper here) that's all but disappeared from New York. (There are more in Brooklyn, I think.) This Polish diner has gentrified a bit (oat bran pancakes? Please!), and is a couple of bucks more expensive than other such joints, but it must be seen. No one in the East Village doesn't eat here!

Yaffa Café (97 St. Marks Place) My friends demanded I include this one, but beware: though this is one of the original East Village cafés, and therefore a legend in its own time, the food's ultra-"natural." Not my bag.

SHOPPING

Make no mistake: New York is the shopping mecca of the world. If you can't find it here, it just can't be found.

Need I tell you about the department stores? All have such great publicity chiefs that you know all about them no matter where you live. For the record, Macy's is the largest store in the world, and has visibly upgraded its image in the past decade; its immenseness deserves a visit, though taking a Tylenol before entering the store is highly recommended. And despite the upscaling, the clientele still tends to be rude and less than soigné, except in the high-priced designer boutiques. Bloomingdale's certainly has the most "New York" reputation, though local trendies never set foot here; it's mainly reserved for tourists and uptowners who think it's "chic." (The store is an unnavigable maze, and even if I liked their merchandise, would be too baffled to shop here.) Saks Fifth Avenue is more genteel, though hardly trendy; Bergdorf Goodman, following the demise of Altman's and Bonwit's (alas!), is the only place of gentility left; and high-fashion women shouldn't miss the hysteria that is Henri Bendel. But all of these places overlook the attention of those of us who live downtown.

That said, let's turn our attention to the prime shopping nabes:

Flatiron/Lower 5th Avenue is the hot, new commercial area in town, and in practically no time has taken off like wildfire. Paul Smith, the excellent English clothier, was one of the first to set up shop here; Emporio Armani and others soon followed suit, and Sasson just opened a salon. It's also in close proximity to Barney's, with probably the most dazzling single collection of high-fashion clothes in the world; originally for men alone, it now features the Penthouse, for exquisite women's threads. It's gorgeous, but only for those with trust funds or corporate salaries, I'm afraid.

Madison Avenue is the stalwart for upper-crust, international designer fashions, though nothing approaches the avant-garde, and the entire experience is so sedate that it will make you snore. Only if you're into the 20-going-on-50 look.

Soho is no longer the trendy little bohemian district it once was; it's big business now. Only yuppies and well-paid artists live in its lofts, and the restaurants are priced out of bounds. Most of the shoppers come from downtown and the 'burbs, Comme des Garcons, Parachute, agnes b., and all the Japanese shops are here. If you've got gelt, don't miss SoHo; but remember that it's priced out-of-sight.

The East Village, dear as it is to our heart, never really took off as a commercial center, mostly due to the burgeoning rents and empty pockets of its residents. Still, you will want to pursue the stores that are here— some of which are great—while making the rounds. St. Marks between 3rd Avenue and Avenue A is key, with the greatest concentration of retail activity going on between 2nd and 3rd Avenues. (The venerable Trash and Vaudeville and Manic Panic are here.) Also, 7th Street between 3rd Avenue and Avenue A deserves a look-see, with the best shops between 1st Avenue and Avenue A. Finally, don't miss 109 St. Mark's Place, owned by dazzling Milanese Gloria Gabe; recently expanded, it's the grande dame of the neighborhood, offering wares by both local designers and bigger names.

The Upper West Side, once no-man's land, is now the home residential and nightlife base for haut-yups, gay and straight. Columbus and Amsterdam Avenues, beginning at 68th Street and going on up, are the boulevards of note here. One store, Charivari, has several branches, divided into men's, women's, sportswear, etc., and has exquisite stuff—though again, at heady prices indeed. While those of us who live on the Lower East Side absolutely never go there (note the dearth of restaurant choices listed here), it's very much a part of the New York experience, and is thus meritorious of an afternoon walk. But why is it when yuppies buy a $1,000 Japanese ensemble, they always have the wrong haircut and shoes?

There are also several tourist meccas—Herald Center, South Street Seaport—but they're too vile to talk about here. Go only if you want to see fatsos from Milwaukee clad in t-shirts proclaiming, "I (heart) New York." Yikes!

NIGHTLIFE

It was but a few years ago that *Village Voice* writer Michael Musto—whose weekly "La Dolce Musto" column chronicles the kaleidoscope of Manhattan's after-dark whirl—declared "downtown is dead." Journalistic hyperbole, yes, but also a telling comment on the then-flagging "below 14th Street" scene. And not just in clubland, but in fashion, music, and their related components.

Musto's *Weltschmerz* pretty much reflected the mood of all of us who lived through the headiness of the late

'70s/early '80s halcyon days (and nights). Believe me, nothing now compares with the fun of seeing Blondie, Television, and the Ramones at places like Max's and CBGB's, or dancing till dawn to the new music at the Mudd Club or Hurrah's. And who could forget a then Pat Benatar-like singer named Madonna Ciccone at the Park Row on Houston Street? (My personal favorite night from that era was the US debut of Poly Styrene and X-Ray Spec at CBGB, a show which was opened by a platform-and-hot-pants clad babe twirling a baton and lip-synching to "These Boots Were Made For Walkin'".)

Later, in the postpunk rainbow days, we had Danceteria (four floors of major fun), Lucky Strike, the Red Bar, and Area. But nightlife really reached its peak—and already began losing some of its irreverence—with the inception of the Palladium's Mike Todd Room. Those of us with VIP invites whisked past hoi polloi to rub shoulders with other downtown superstars; and no one glittered as brightly as Dianne Brill, dubbed "the Queen of the Night." But by then, nightlife had already progressed from outré, avant-garde status to media darling, and what was once truly underground had become—at least to some extent—mainstream. (Even so, we always had places like Save the Robots and The World in the bowels of the Lower East Side, joints where even the most intrepid slumming yuppie dared not tread.)

Today, New York's "alternative" nightlife is on the upswing again. True, we don't have the proliferation of places once extant, nor is there the wild burst of energy of the "early" days. But New York after dark is still the most exciting state of mind in the world; long may she wave!

One final note: nothing is more volatile than the whims of clubsters in New York, so you'll necessarily want to update the following list with some quick fact-checking of your own. Doing so is easy; just read Michael Musto's column in the *Voice*, or pick up the latest edition of the excellent and politically on-target *Paper* magazine, which always has the dish on groovy clubs.

Clubs

Dance your ass off and look fabulous at:

MONDAY

Canal Bar (Spring St. & Greenwich Ave.) Steve Blush (ex- of the semilegendary Carmelita's) spins groovy sounds for a motley collection of bohos, club rats, Eurotrash, and yups. But what else are ya gonna do on Monday night?

TUESDAY

Larry Tee's Love Machine (Union Square at 17th St.) Ultrahip young assortment of FIT students, other fashionites, club recidivists, et al; girls galore, but fewer straight boys. Drag queens and boys-in-underwear rule entertainment scene. Trendy plus.

WEDNESDAY

Nell's (14th St. bet 7th and 8th Avenues) The club hasn't regained its haut-trendy reputation, but with a dearth of other options, Wednesday night is back "in" again here. DJ spins reggae, hip-hop, classics, and more.

THURSDAY

MK (204 Fifth Ave.) Not the bastion of cool it once was, swanky MK has reserved Thursday for the downtown straight crowd. Drinks are priced outta sight to match English Gentleman's club decor. Bands, sometimes.

Nightrain at The Building (51 W. 26th St.) Underdecorated hip-hop rap club is coolest tonight. Sometimes unsavory urban crowd.

FRIDAY

There hasn't been a damned thing to do in New York on Friday night since Charlton's Bar closed years ago. Have a late dinner with friends in the East Village, then stop into any dive and get drunk. That's what we locals do.

SATURDAY

Deep (The secretest new underground spot in New York; I'd have my arms and legs broken if I revealed the address. If you're cool enough, you'll pry the logistics from locals. Hint: it's in the bowels of the East Village/Lower

East Side.) Psychedelic/hip-hop cum old rock rules. Very late, very trendy, and very fun.

Roxy (515 W. 18th St.) Susanne Bartsch, the Swiss Miss who now rules Gotham's nightlife scene, has come up with a cure for the Saturday night blues. The new hot night; everything from models to avant-garders to urban kids. Not to be missed.

Sound Factory (27th between 10th and 11th aves.) Don't even think of going before 4:00 A.M., and it's open till God knows what time the next day. No liquor (but other mind-changers galore), house music rules, mainly (but not exclusively) gay; everyone from aristocrats to Bronx babies winds up here.

SUNDAY

Nell's is arguably the straight place to go, though many hetero ultratrendies tend to prefer the Sunday night gay places, notably Mars and the Pyramid.

Pyramid 2000 (Avenue A between 6th and 7th) is an East Village institution, the longest-running club in our part of town. At one time not too long ago, Sunday night at the Pyramid was talked about all week long; it was a neighborhood gathering, the town courtyard of the Lower East Side. Arguably a gay night, it nonetheless attracted with-it folks of all races, sexual orientations, and other societal denominators. Hilarious Hapi Phace has ruled the night for years, and such performers as Ann Magnuson, Lypsinka, and Ethyl Eichelberger made their names here. Alas, the new owner has been accused of homophobia, and the Sunday night crowd has dwindled to a fraction of its former strength and size. Yet—call me a sentimentalist—I have faith that Sunday at the Pyramid will rise like a phoenix from the ashes and once again become the coolest place in New York. So there!

A final note: I regret to note that the East Village, once filled with zillions of much-fun bars, offers practically no decent watering holes at this time. Places like the Holiday and Aztec, once stalwarts, now attract a young, fairly suburban crowd; even the venerable Gold Bar has lost its original clientele. As an alternative, many locals simply meet at East Village restaurants or cafés; of these, the Café Orlin, 7A, Mary Ann's Distrito Federal, and the Sidewalk Café are key. (More upscale, and less neighborhoody, is the crowd at Jerry's 103.)

Gay

Private Eyes (21st St. between 5th and 6th avenues) The closest N.Y. has to an L.A. gay bar: white, sterile, pumped up pretty boys. Strippers (unraunchy) sometimes.

Pyramid (see "Nightlife" above; look in *Village Voice* for current info on gay nights)

Quick! (see "Nightlife" above; gay day is Thursday)

The Bar (4th St. and 2nd Ave.) The first gay bar in the East Village; has lost clientele to the Tunnel, but for boho boys, it's still packed on Friday nights.

The Works (Columbus Ave. at 81st St.) Upper West Side (that is, nontrendy) cruise bar.

Tunnel Bar (7th Street and 1st Ave.) Dark little dive that's now the darling of the East Village (read: boho) crowd.

Uncle Charlie's (Greenwich Ave. south of 12th St.) The shopping mall of gay bars. Leading meat rack; some hipsters, but mainly uncool and/or suburban boys.

PHILADELPHIA

I've been harboring a theory about Philadelphia's image problem since I was ten. Here it is: 90 percent of the city's bad rep comes from its name. To me, it sounds like an incurable skin disease, something attended to in 15th century France.

But if you strip away the name and the local accent (the ugliest case of regionalism on the East Coast), you'll discover there's quite a lot to like. Few cities anywhere can match Philly's quaint colonial architecture, at least in Center City and Society Hill; the rest of the city is pretty much of an aesthetic mess. Add the world-renowned Art Museum and the thriving restaurant scene, and Philly can be downright romantic at times.

To my mind, Philadelphia always looks best in the rain when it resembles a movie set from Revolutionary War days.

There are gorgeous brownstones throughout Center City, but don't miss the best—on Spruce and Locust Streets between 20th and 21st. (I'm sure you'll find a favorite block to call your own.)

Philadelphia suffers from the same "shadow of New York syndrome" that Baltimore, Boston, and D.C. do, and in some ways this reputation is well-deserved. I lived here for two years while in grad school at Penn, and quickly tired of the city with its relative provincialism and limited after-dark scene. Yet now that I don't have to reside there, I visit for weekends and really enjoy the city.

Philadelphia's student population has produced a small, yet vital, alternative scene. There are any number of places to hear live music (though these are also plagued by a contingent of aged hippies who, alas, have nowhere else to go), a great experimental theatre house (the TLA), and bookstores galore—including several with a New Age bent. Interestingly enough, I recently found myself in one such emporium—replete with incense and Andreas Vollenweider tapes—which also featured a section labeled "Finance."

The nightlife scene is relatively limited; as in most cities outside New York, Los Angeles, and San Francisco, there are only one or two clubs where the "in"- telligentsia hang.

Philadelphia's tourist sites can easily be covered in a couple of days, unless you're a die-hard American history fan. Spend the first day taking a walking tour (begin on grand Rittenhouse Square, surely one of the loveliest city parks in the United States), then head east toward Society Hill to see the Liberty Bell (and coexisting horde of bored kids).

Philly is the country's fifth-largest city, but it's primarily composed of working-class (and poor) neighborhoods, so outside the core of Center City, the number of attractions is small. (The wealth is concentrated in the suburbs, particularly the famed Main Line.) On day two, do the Art Museum and Italian Market, and you'll pretty much have seen it all. (I can hear the Philadelphia Visitors Bureau screaming as I write.)

Gastronomes can easily justify a weekend in Philly for the varied restaurant scene. Add tickets to Riccardo Muti's symphony or to a production of the excellent Walnut Street Theatre (one of the East Coast's most esteemed regional showplaces), and the city becomes a wonderfully accessible urban weekend destination—at least if you live anywhere in the stretch from Washington to New York.

One final recommendation: Philadelphia is best visited in the winter or fall; the gorgeous old brownstones and cobbled streets of Society Hill look loveliest at that time. Don't even try to visit in summer; on summer weekends, everyone's "down the shore" (translation: "at a beach in New Jersey"), away from the city's muggy, stifling heat.

GETTING CENTERED

"Philly is so small!" is the familiar refrain of visitors from New York. To be sure, the downtown area, from which you may well have no reason to stray during a weekend trip, is easily covered by foot. Yet the residential zones of this "city of neighborhoods" cover a vast geographical surface. So, unless you plan to explore South Philly (warning: Fabian doesn't live there anymore) or the malls of the city's Northeast, a pocket-sized map is all you need.

Rittenhouse Square marks the elite core of Center City. Whether this landmark or City Hall, at 14th and Broad, signals the actual crux of Philadelphia is immaterial; both are focal points you should know about. Society Hill, rich with federal townhouses and historical sites, lies due east. (To give you an idea of Center City's compactness, it takes no more than 45 minutes to walk from the Delaware to Schuylkill Rivers, which bound downtown.) The other area of town you should visit (especially if you're a student) is West Philly, home to the University of Pennsylvania and Drexel University—as well as MOVE, those darling buds of civil disobedience. (They're still there, I'm told.)

Since Philadelphia's Center City is small, there isn't much room for good, cheap hotels. There are only a couple of inexpensive places right in Center City, and they're basically glorified welfare hotels. Other downtown hotels are very upscale. You're going to have to spend more for lodging here than in almost any American city except New York.

HOTELS

Holiday Inn (4th & Arch) A fine, medium-priced choice. Convenient to historical sites and trendy Old City area. High moderate.

Latham Hotel (135 S. 17th St.; 215/563-7474) Wonderful old European-style hotel with splendid Old World facade. Rooms are lovely, and most of them have great views; relaxed and unstuffy. Expensive.

Quality Inn Center City (501 N. 22nd St.; 215/568-3636) Central to Art Museum and Voodoo Club. No beauty, but a decent, affordable contender. Moderate.

St. Charles Hotel (1935 Arch St.; 215/567-5651) Very basic, slightly rundown hotel, also near Art Museum. The best—and perhaps only—dirt-cheap entry near downtown.

The Rittenhouse (210 West Rittenhouse Square; 215/732-3364) Brand new hotel and condominium has immediately become *the* prestige hotspot. Gorgeous lobby and rooms, service of the first rank. "210" Restaurant is an expense accounter's must. A joy! Very expensive.

Warwick (17th & Locust sts.; 215/735-6000) Elegant old Philly hotel, more than a touch of class. (Foreign heiresses attending Penn lived here.) A bit stodgy, of course. Expensive.

RESTAURANTS

Alouette (334 Bainbridge) Wonderfully inventive French/Thai cuisine; intimate, pastel-y decor.

Apropos (211 S. Broad) Nouvelle California cooking with a slight Mediterranean accent. It works!

Astral Plane (1708 Lombard) Cozy, haut-bohemian eatery, famed for its mismatched decor and fine food.

Boathouse Row Bar (210 Rittenhouse Square, in Rittenhouse Hotel) High-yuppie crowd, inventive finger foods.

Brera (615 South St.) My favorite restaurant in town: small, postmodern (replete with changing art), and the best Milanese cooking you'll ever eat. Very trendy.

Brera Due (Bainbridge) A café, really, with light repasts. Like its mother restaurant, hosts a very with-it crowd.

Café Nola (328 South St.) Philly's premier Cajun/Creole spot. No longer *the* trend, but great food nonetheless.

Carolina's (261 S. 20) Updated Continental, usually with piano and jazz. On the yup side.

Chameleon (1519 Walnut) Another personal favorite: gourmet cafeteria cum catering business. Wonderful and very cheap—the perfect place to eat alone.

Ciboulette (1312 Spruce) French Provincial at its best. Tasting menu ($60) is a wonderful splurge.

Commissary (1710 Sansom) A Center City tradition. Upstairs: USA Café; downstairs: cafeteria (desserts are the best!).

Cutters (2005 Market) Semitrendy; more important, open very late. Serviceable food.

Jake's (4365 Main) American-based menu (seasonally adjusted for freshness) in newly trendy working-class nabe on the edge of town. Worth it if you have the time.

Le Bec-Fin (1523 Walnut) Philadelphia's most famous restaurant, internationally acclaimed. *Haute cuisine Franchaise*; very pricey indeed.

Le Bus (3402 Sansom) Light entrees, pasta, cafeteria-style. Near University of Pennsylvania campus.

Metropolis (1515 Locust) American regional specialties in Fritz Lang-inspired decor. Casual, upbeat.

16th Street Bar and Grill (264 S. 16 St.) Very casual, inexpensive, Mediterranean-based menu here.

Susanna Foo (1512 Walnut) Voted the country's best Chinese restaurant by *Esquire* magazine. Inventive, sumptuous, and really worth the price. (Who sez *I* paid?)

White Dog Café (3420 Sansom) Another Penn/Drexel haunt. Lovely brownstone setting, daring American cuisine.

SHOPPING

Because Philadelphians (unlike New Yorkers) don't spend all their money on rent, they've got bucks to burn on clothes. Perhaps this is why there are some wonderful places to shop. Not as many outlets of the avant-garde as a New York or Paris, but enough to keep even shopaholics busy on a weekend jaunt.

Prime zones are:

Old City, centered on 2nd and 3rd from Market to Race, has a few offbeat shops, though this area never really took off like they thought it would. One strong calling card is this district's several highly inventive furniture design studios, which have recently been hailed in the national press. Finally, bargain-crazed readers will not want to miss Franklin Mills, billed as the "world's largest outlet mall." Far from the center of town in Philly's vast Northeast, it really is an off-price mecca, including wares from some very top names. (Rumor has it Saks Fifth Avenue is opening a discount branch soon—but mum's the word!)

South Street between 2nd and 8th. Shops run the gamut from punk leather to haute couture, with a couple of upper-mid range places like Matinique thrown in for good measure. Best bet: Urban Guerilla, with witty, funky clothes for women and men. (The whole strip is a six-minute walk, so I'll let you discover the rest for yourself.)

Walnut Street between Broad Street and 20th. Beginning at the Bellevue Hotel (which boasts Philly's first Gucci shop—ooh!) and continuing west, this strip features a great men's shop (Allure) and (on 18th, just off the strip) women's store, Knit Wit. Don't miss Nan Duskin, a longtime Philly institution (ever-so-refined, but surprisingly updated as well) in its new home in the Rittenhouse Hotel.

NIGHTLIFE

As mentioned, this isn't Philly's strong suit. Still, there are a few places to play; my picks are:

Clubs

Bacchanal (1320 South St.) The best of the live music clubs, though the old-hippie market alluded to above is a force here. Go for the groups.

Black Banana (3rd and Race Sts.) Still going crazy after all these years, though with new competition in town, some luster lost. Still Philly's only real after-hours place to go, a recommendation unto itself.

Polo Bay (Warwick Hotel, 17th and Locust Sts.) *Not cool*, but the premier yuppies-in-heat haunt. (Don't say I didn't warn you in the strongest of terms!)

Revival (22 South 3rd St.) Along with Voodoo (below),

the most happening crowd in town. Music ranges from acid to rock to house.

Roxxi (602 S. 2nd St.) Art deco environment is far more interesting than the (mainly South Philly) crowd.

Voodoo (2121 Arch St.) Philly's newest hip venue, now drawing Revival's crowd. Who will win? Only time will tell.

Gay

Kurt's (1229 Chestnut) Turned-up collars, gay crowd. '70s disco lives in the City of Brotherly Love!

Woody's (202 S. 13th) Always-popular watering hole, bit-of-everything crowd.

SAN FRANCISCO

Is San Francisco the most delicious city in the world? It's a close call: the blue ribbon may go to Paris, buy why split hairs when the gorgeous City by the Bay is on our own shores?

Comparing San Francisco (never "Frisco," please!) to the French capital is not off base, by the way; there's no more European city in the United States. And not just by dint of its innate sophistication and beauty, but because San Franciscans are about the most epicurean, sensual lot you could ever hope to meet. The city's "sinful" past is no secret, but it goes further than that: quite simply, locals are true lovers of life, reveling equally in their spectacular natural surroundings and in the city's heady cultural, social, and—yes!—spiritual whirl.

People here work, to be sure, yet they also understand the importance of play. The meaningless pursuit of yuppie ideals is not entirely foreign, but few budding capitalists succumb to the rigors of a N.Y.-style 14-hour workday. And why should they, when their city's range of nocturnal goings-on—from a dizzying array of restaurants to an intensely fun nightlife—beckons to leave the office behind?

In many ways, San Francisco seems to be a nation unto itself, certainly a foreign entity with respect to the rest of the state, which, outside of most of Los Angeles, is as hick and backwoodsy as Arkansas and views San Francisco as a haven for "hippies and fags."

The reason, of course, is that San Francisco boasts a long and well-deserved reputation as a center for disaffected intelligentsia, bohemians, down-and-outs, and societal misfits of any ilk. The century-old influx of "weirdos and foreigners" has forged a spirit of social tolerance that could well serve as a model for the rest of the country—and, in fact, the world.

From your standpoint, one would be hard-pressed to conjure up a city (even in the imagination!) with more for the visitor to do. One could easily spend a week getting to know the city's neighborhoods alone; there's hardly a block that doesn't offer something of culinary, architectural, or social interest. (The nabes of note are listed in "Getting Centered," below). But whatever you do, don't rush—San Francisco is made to be savored, just like the exquisite coffee at one of its many cafés.

Thus, this advice: arm yourself with reading matter, stationery, Walkman, and set out for the day. It's good to have a general plan, but in a city with so many lures, let your senses lead the way. That's what the locals do, and it's really the only way to explore the beloved City by the Bay.

GETTING CENTERED

Though its population is less than 750 thousand, and New Yorkers inevitably say, "it's such a small town," San Francisco is not a city defined by a finite downtown. If anything, you'll feel the city is bigger than it is, simply because there are so many different parts of town you'll want to see. Since San Francisco's public transportation system is probably the most efficient one in the country, a car is not required, though it's not a bad idea to rent one if you plan to spend a few days in Marin, Mendocino, the Napa Valley, Santa Cruz, or anywhere else out of town.

There is a "downtown," though it refers usually to the smallish but vital financial district. Else, one would do well to consider Union Square as the city's downtown, surrounded as it is by the usual contingent of upscale department stores, airline offices, and boutiques. In many cities, this would be an area of cursory interest, but like everything else here, it has—despite hordes of tourists—its own special charm. (Somehow, the frantic consumerism is not quite so great as it is on, say, Fifth Avenue in New York.)

Chinatown abuts Union Square; enter via the gateway on Grant Street. The largest Chinese center of population outside the Orient, San Francisco's Chinatown is not just an EPCOT-style tourist trap, but a teeming, vital city unto its own. (It's also the filthiest, most overcrowded part of town, and to some degree run by the Chinese mafia and gangs.) But that's all pretty much hidden, so there's no danger to the tourist here. Since Chinatown is fairly well composed of vegetable markets, restaurants, and souvenir shops, the sophisticated traveler won't spend much time here, but it's worth an hour-and-a-half at least. And just for the record, my favorite restaurant is the slightly upscale, quasi-healthy, Brandy Ho's.

North Beach, the old Italian quarter centered around gorgeous Washington Square (with Rittenhouse Square and Central Park, one of my favorites in the United States) should be certified a national gem, and continues to serve as the lifeline of the Bay Area's large Italian-American community. The Caffé Trieste is world-famous for its coffee and opera—not to mention desserts!—but I'd rather spend time perusing the delicacies in the small Old World delicatessens, which flavor North Beach with a distinct, made-in-Italy air.

Telegraph Hill, upon which sits Coit Towers, adjoins North Beach, and remains one of the prime residential areas, especially because of its apartments' unparalleled view of the city and bay. Unless you're incredibly hardy, don't even try to walk up the winding road to the Tower;

take a car, bus, or cab. You may think you're doing well, but the next day, your calves and ankles will hurt so badly you will hardly be able to walk. Believe me!

Fisherman's Wharf is, I suppose, something every visitor must see, though the hordes of tacky tourist shops (and tourists, of course) will probably have you screaming fast. So go, but don't plan on being able to stomach the proceedings for more than about half an hour.

Pacific Heights is the bona-fide yuppie (and, in neighboring Laurel Heights, old money) district, yet even yups have a sense of style and humor here, so don't be scared away. Fillmore, the main shopping drag, has a wonderful movie theater, a couple of great bookstores, and some upscale-trendy shops. It's a neighborhood that's worth strolling through.

Haight-Ashbury (more familiarly known as "the Haight") is indeed the hippie hangout of yore; burnouts can still be found, but today it hosts a youth counterculture all its own. Though it's gone slightly upscale by dint of an upsurge of restaurants and shops (even in the "Lower Haight," near the Western Addition/Fillmore black ghetto), used record and clothing shops still abound—as, of course, do the requisite granola cafés. The Haight is also a sought-after place to live among the nontraditional crowd because it's usually sunny (each district in San Francisco has a microclimate all its own) and its Victorian flats are usually breathtakingly huge. (One bedroom is larger than most apartments in New York.)

The Castro/Upper Market area is the heartbeat of

San Francisco's well-known gay community. It's not a ghetto, however, but a celebration, and people of all walks of life can be found cruising down Castro Street on a Sunday afternoon. (It's also the site of the city's world famous Halloween parade.) I had heard that the Castro had suffered badly from the AIDS epidemic, but my impression is that this medical emergency has caused the gay population to cohere and grow into a major political, spiritual, and social force.

Finally, "the Avenues"—the working- to middle-class neighborhood of the Sunset and Richmond on the Pacific Coast—have their own special, "normal" charm (but remember TV's *Twin Peaks*). The Richmond is the more interesting of the two, since it boasts Clement Street, a spirited shopping/restaurant street, on which you'll find practically any kind of ethnic food (though Eastern European is more predominant here). The Sunset has a reputation for being quiet and staid, but there are actually some scenemakers—rock heartthrob Chris Isaak, for one—who choose to live away from the central city's dizzy scene. There's also one great art cinema, the Surf, which can be reached on the N Judah tram line.

HOTELS

Campton Place Hotel (340 Stockton; 415/781-5555)
A bit stuffy, but a fine, upscale hotel for those on expense accounts; more for the business than tourist crowd. And the restaurant is nationally ranked. Very expensive.

Canterbury-Whitehall Inn (750 Sutter; 415/474-6464) An old favorite, not glitzy, but a charming old hotel, and pricewise, it can't be beat. Moderate.

El Cortez (500 Geary; 415/775-5000) Funky old stalwart, '30s-ish style, very central, and probably the cheapest decent place to stay for budget visitors. Low moderate.

Hotel Diva (440 Geary; 415/885-0200) High-tech, Italianate decor makes this *the* fashion hotel in town. For the trendy traveler, this place is it. Expensive.

Hotel Nikko (222 Mason; 415/394-1111) Of the large new hotels, the ultramodern Nikko can't be beat; takes the anonymity of a Grand Hyatt and makes it an art. Very expensive.

Kensington Park (450 Post; 415/788-6400) From the same people who brought you the Diva, this less-fashionable, but equally central and less expensive smallish hotel can hardly be beat for the price. Very helpful staff, too. Expensive.

Mark Hopkins (One Nob Hill; 415/392-3434) Atop Nob Hill, it's probably the best-known hotel in town; certainly the Top of the Mark bar is a standard meeting place. One of the country's great hotels. Very expensive.

Phoenix (601 Eddy; 415/776-1380) For the rock 'n' roll, avant-garde crowd, there's no better place anywhere to stay. A former no-name motel has been transformed into a high-California, L.A.-style hangout reminiscent of the old Tropicana in West Hollywood. Piped-in tropical bird noises by scenemaking pool. The best! (I saw Sinead O'Connor here!) Moderate.

Seal Rock Inn (545 Point Lobos; 415/752-8000) Not real central, but right on the ocean; a perfect romantic hideaway, with faux-rococo decor to boot. Low moderate.

Standford Court (905 California; 415/989-3500) Perhaps more elegant than even the Mark, it's a center for visiting dignitaries, haut-business types, and more. If you're into European-type elegance, this is for you. Very expensive.

RESTAURANTS

Alejandro's (1840 Clement) Two things are certain: you'll have to wait, and the Spanish/Peruvian food will keep you coming back for more. In the Richmond, but get there by hook or crook; it's one of those authentically local restaurants that couldn't be anywhere but San Francisco. Tapas is heaven on earth!

Bahia (41 Franklin) The key Brazilian place in town; dancing, too, but the food and nonstop energy are alone worth the trip. *Muito bom!*

Border Café & Cantina (1192 Folsom) Tex-Mex food and decor, South of Market (if not the border). Avoid on weekends, but cool crowd during the week.

Caffè Sport (574 Green) Not trendy, just the best Italian food in North beach—quite a mouthful! Family-style seating (usually, twice a night, so call first). A great place to go with a small group of friends.

Campton Place (340 Stockton) Nouvelle American at its best, one of the top-rated restaurants in the country. Upscale-trendy, but worth a splurge.

Chez Panisse (1517 Shattuck, Berkeley) One of the best restaurants in the country, presided over by now-famous Alice Waters, whose California-style nouvelle cuisine quickly became a national trend. Ultrafresh ingredients, gorgeously served. Expensive, but worth it; anyone who is interested in food should stop here.

Embarko (100 Brannan) South-of-Market eatery, Casabalanca-esque decor, lively crowd. Ethnic American fare rules.

Golden Turtle (2211 Van Ness) Vietnamese par excellence, and a local ethnic gem you'll not find anywhere else. (Avoid the new one on Van Ness, and schlep out to the Richmond for authenticity's sake.) One of those places I fit in every time I'm in town.

Hamburger Mary's (1582 Folsom) An institution, and rightly so. Avoid on weekends, when suburbanites rule, but during the week it's still a very funky crowd, and was cool before the rest of South of Market was "in." A must.

Just Desserts (Around town) A quasi-institution, almost

requisite after a spicy meal. Cozy, informal setting, and the best ole desserts in town. Or go and stake out a spot by yourself.

La Rondalla (901 Valencia) No cool-minded traveler could come to San Francisco without stopping here. The decor is year-round Christmas lights, the food plentiful, and the margaritas could stop a mule. Funksters abound, especially late, mixing with Chicano Mission crowd. ¡*Muy festivo!*

Little Joe's (532 Broadway) The classic location has moved, but it's Little Joe's just the same. Huge, great Italian dishes—*robusto* to the max! Utterly informal, an odd collection of tourists and locals, but so San Francisco that it can hardly be missed.

Manora's Thai Cuisine (1600 Folsom) A Thai art bar? Well, almost; the authentic adornments only enhance the flavorful food, among the best Thai you'll eat. Devotés of Siamese will not want to overlook this one.

Ma Tante Sumi (4243 18th St.) Franco-Japanese-Californian menu in a bistro setting, it's one of the most innovative—and best—kitchens in town. This new-L.A. cuisine heads north!

Miss Pearl's Jam House (601 Larkin, in Phoenix Hotel) The name alone invites a visit, no? High-funk Caribbean decor and innovative same food, priced low, and always crowded—a loud, but very hip scene. Do not miss!

Rings (1131 Folsom) Art, mesquite, pink decor—you know the scene. Still, it's one of SoMa's best, and one of the trendiest places in town.

Stars (150 Redwood) Trend-o restaurant of long-standing, innovative menu. Stylemakers mix with elite business types; best as the night wears on.

Swan Oyster Depot (1517 Polk) Gorgeous, old marble bar, some tables, superfresh seafood of all kinds. A great place to dine solo. The food's the thing, and is it ever!

Tadich Grill (240 California) Talk about authentic: this one's been here since 1849. Business-y crowd, yet the Gold Rush decor and sumptuous sea fare are worth putting up with any distractions. Very old-time San Francisco, thus an obligatory pit-stop.

Taxi (374 11th St.) A former warehouse, now the darling of the trendy set, this wonderful place serves excellent California cuisine. Upscale artiste.

U.S. Restaurant (431 Columbus) More subdued and more local than Little Joe's—thus "hipper," I must say—it has the same *abbondanza*, usually perfect, Italian food. The untouched Little Italy decor alone is worth the trip. Another absolute must.

Washington Square Bar and Grill (1707 Powell) Ostensibly a journalist's hangout, it's certainly North Beach's best "upscale" restaurant. Trendy among upscale types, yet informal enough to be enjoyed by all.

Yet Wah (2140 Clement) Worth the ride to the Richmond District for what's generally considered the best Chinese in town. And in San Francisco, that's saying a lot!

Zuni Café (1658 Market) One of the city's perpetually "in" places, a special favorite among the Haight/Castro crowd. French/Italian specialties done cum mesquite, many think it's just the best food in town. It's certainly a restaurant you should try not to miss.

SHOPPING

San Francisco has about everything a shopper could want, and more; fashionwise, it's every bit the equal of L.A. and New York.

Union Square is the traditional upscale shopping area, boasting excellent department stores (Macy's California, Neiman Marus, Saks, Nordstrom's, and I. Magnin) in a greater concentration than anywhere else in the States. And don't balk (I hate department stores), because the range of merchandise is as hip as it comes. In addition to the typical international boutique suspects, you'll find Wilkes Bashford, which along with Barney's in N.Y. and Fred Segal in L.A., is probably *the* place for men and women with money and taste to shop. All the Japanese and European designers, along with some up-and-coming American ones, are here. Great duds, with price tags to match.

Crocker Galleria (50 Post), right near Union Square, is

a pleasant urban mall with everything from top-of-the-line boutiques like Versace to more standard, Limited/Rodier fare. Worth a look-see.

Fillmore Street (between Jackson & Sutter in Pacific Heights) is an upscale shopping artery with well-merchandised, well-designed shops. A superlovely street, worth a stroll unto itself.

Haight Street, especially near Golden Gate park (but now filtering all the way down to Divisadero) is the traditional nontraditional place to shop. Punk hair salons, funky boutiques, and even a bowling alley grace San Francisco's quirkiest commercial strip. You simply can't come to town and not do the Haight, so plan on spending a good long afternoon here.

San Francisco Centre (865 Market) is a new urban mall that's been winning raves. Slants upscale, though less than avant-garde; still, you should take a look when you're in the nabe.

24th Street in the Noe Valley, a nice walk from the Castro, is *très* San Francisco: granola cafes, used record stores, and upscale kids' shops abound. Still, this laidback, friendly feeling is what San Francisco is all about, so don't fail to wend your way here.

Union Street (between Steiner & Gough) is also less than prophetic, and can be touristy as hell; and since it's in the Marina, yuppies abound. Still and all, this is San Francisco, and it's one of the prettiest shopping streets, so go during the week to miss the weekend traffic.

Upper Market between Sanchez and Castro is a booming, new commercial center, that continues onto Castro itself. (18th Street is a storefront street, too.) Everything from innovative young designers (at California on Market) to funky urban gear, and then some; a casual, unhurried place to shop.

NIGHTLIFE

San Francisco has the hippest night scene outside of New York, and because it's less rigidly stratified—and certainly less expensive—some may argue that it's even more fun. That debate aside, even the haughtiest nightbird will find a haunt that fits into his or her scene. The best:

Clubs

Bahia Tropical Brazilian Club (1600 Market) is a mixed bag—all varieties of race, class, and sexual orientation congregate here. And why not; the food's fine, and the Brazilian performers (or tapes) are a welcome change from the hip-hop staples. Not supertrendy, but fun nonetheless.

Club Uranus (401 Sixth St.) Sunday night only, it's the place to hang with San Francisco's hippest boys and girls. Slants gay, but all the coolies go. And who could resist the name?

CLVB DV8 (55 Natoma) Often credited with igniting the mid-'80s San Francisco club renaissance, the DV8 shines on, though a slightly less decadent version of its original self. The faux-Roman-cum-Keith Haring-designed club plays the best music in town, and is open till 4 A.M. on weekends—the later, the hipper.

DNA Lounge (375 11th St.) Avant-garde clientele, often with live music, shows, and impromptu performances of any kind. Open till 4:00 A.M. at all times; more local crowd during the week.

Firehouse 7 (3160 16th St.) Youngish crowd, certainly less hip than DV8 or DNA, but good music all the same. Also, it's free, thus perhaps worth a look-see; the crowd changes every night.

Hotel Utah (500 Fourth St.) Your usual collection of South of Market types; one of the stalwarts of the scene. Good from early evening on; a great, funky beer pitstop.

I-Beam (1748 Haight) In the early '80s, this was the place to see new English bands; today, the I-Beam carries on, with different themes/clientele every night. Call first to see if the night is straight or gay.

Kennel Club (628 Divisadero) Live rock rules; a down and dirty place where you may hear your favorite alternative bands. Check the *Bay Guardian* for schedules.

Lipps Underground Club (201 9th St.) Open virtually

all night long, it's the new place for the fashion-victim-ized (or just plain stoned) crowd. Open till 3 A.M. during the week, if you're still in the mood after all else is closed.

Nightbreak (1821 Haight) An ongoing Haight institution, usually with bands, and always with a small dance floor; alternative sounds rule. Wednesday night is reserved for lesbian "Female Trouble" night—perhaps the best-named party in town!

Noc Noc (557 Haight) Ushered in the Haight's nightlife renaissance and still a factor. Intimate, with every type from butch boys to gender-benders.

Paradise Lounge (1501 Folsom) Expanded from its first incarnation, there are now a couple of levels, featuring everything from garage bands to poetry readings. The hippest crowd in town; mostly straight, but gays welcome in force. A place to hang out anytime at all (open from 4:00 P.M. on).

Townsend (177 Townsend) Former warehouse now a huge dance hall; bands, sometimes, other times, progressive rock. Open till 4:00 A.M. on weekends. New, but looks to be hot.

Gay

Atlas (715 Harrison) Friday night special; too soon to be called (though the talent—porn stars, etc.—does not compare well with that at Uranus and Colossus). Tell me how it turns out.

Colossus (1015 Folsom) Saturdays only, a supercool dance spot in an otherwise Godawful club. Be there or be square!

Crystal Pistol (20th & Valencia) Thursdays and Fridays, it's '70s-disco retrospective time. Gay on Thursday, mixed Friday, but always super, supercool. Go!

Midnight Sun (4067 18th St.) One of the oldest video bars in the country, and always packed, with a mixed gay crowd, though less trendy than you'd probably like. Vids are more Stevie Nicks than avant-garde, sad to say.

Screw (14th & Guerrero) A new Saturday night spot in a rowdy old bar; Doc Martens and leather only, please. Your prototypically wonderful South of Market dive!

The Box (628 Divisadero) Racially mixed gay dance hall that jams on Thursdays and Saturdays with rap and hip-hop. A very happening scene, trendy to the core.

The Stud (9th & Harrison) The Stud, alas, is a mere spectre of its former self—but since this was, until recently, one of the coolest bars in the world, that's saying quite a lot. It's still the place to go for postpunk gay boys during the week, and hip straights happen in, too.

SAN JUAN

In 1950, the opening of the Caribe Hilton marked the almost immediate transformation of Puerto Rico from a sleepy little island to a major tourist attraction. And, for about 30 years after that, San Juan remained an international mecca for lovers of the sun.

For better or worse, the city is no longer a beacon to the touring elite. Frankly, it lacks the Episcopalian trade who frequent Barbados, the yuppies of St. Maarten, or the Frenchy feel of Martinique. In fact, it is a lot like any Sun Belt city in the United States: finding indigenous cuisine is much more difficult than finding soggy Big Macs.

Of course, if you're devoted to the sun, it doesn't much matter where you go. But lovers of the social whirl, be forewarned: San Juan is no longer the darling of the international jet set—or even the American upper-middle-class.

Yet San Juan is still a cheap and easy winter get-away and offers sufficient diversions for a couple of days or three. After that, unless you decide to go "out on the Island"—the insider's phrase for anywhere other than San Juan—I can't promise you'll not grow wildy bored.

Yes, Old San Juan is charming (though the hucksters and bums are not); but it can easily be seen in an afternoon. The old fort is scenic, but it won't take up much of your time. So my advice is to stay the weekend, then hit the road (either to the picturesque towns of Ponce and Mayaguez, or back home).

Beach towns—even big ones—tend to lack sights and culture, and that's pretty much the rule here (Raul Julia's omnipresent television spots to the contrary). But when you add the American influence, even the exoticism of a French or Dutch island is wanting in San Juan. More-over, to a New Yorker, a Puerto Rican isn't exactly a *rara avis*; more than once, I felt like I was back in the East Village.

There are, of course, some very good restaurants and a slightly amusing—though less than tantalizing—nightlife. In all, San Juan is a pleasant enough winter escape, and sometimes, that's all you really need.

IN TRANSIT

American Airlines is the way to go, with more flights to San Juan than any other carrier. From San Juan, there are direct flights to Boston, Hartford, New York, Newark, Philadelphia, Baltimore, Washington, D.C., Chicago, Nashville, Orlando, Tampa, Miami, and Dallas.

GETTING CENTERED

No tall order here. San Juan, like most island towns, is primarily residential; the tourist area is very concentrated indeed. El Condado, centered around Ashford Avenue, is a six-minute walk from one end to the other, and if you're like most visitors, you'll probably stay here. The Puerta de Tierra zone is directly to the northwest (nothing here but the Hilton Caribe and Radisson hotels), and Old San Juan lies due west of these.

South of Condado is Miramar, a newly popular hotel area. To Condado's east is Ocean Park, a nice residential neighborhood where you'll find several lovely tourist inns. Southeast of Condado is the Hato Rey business district, and to its southeast is the university town of Rio Piedras. That's about all you need to know.

While San Juan is well serviced by buses, there's no need to become intimately acquainted with them. You'll spend most of your time on the beach, but you can take a relatively inexpensive taxi to wherever you want to go. (If you've come to spend a weekend in the sun, then you can ignore all references to bus routes, *verdad?*)

HOTELS

Atlantic Beach (1 Vendig; 809/721-6900) Functional, central, funky hotel right on Condado Beach. Mixed/gay clientele. Moderate.

Caribe Hilton (Fort San Jeronimo; 809/721-0303) The Hilton first brought tourism to the island 40 years ago. Has lost some luster, but still boasts San Juan's only private beach. Very expensive.

Excelsior (801 Ponce de Leon; 809/721-7400). Nicest midpriced hotel in town (but no beach, alas).

Radisson San Juan (Muñoz Rivera; 809/729-2929) Lovely Art Deco renovation: very tasteful, superquiet for those incognito.

Ramada El Convento (100 Cristo; 809/723-9020) Perhaps the only hotel right in Old San Juan. Far from beaches, but local color galore. Moderate.

San Juan (Isla Verde; 809/791-1000) Currently the city's hottest hotel; elegant yet happening, with very high-brow (largely European) clientele. The place to be, though not the most central. Very expensive.

Tanamá (1 Joffre; 809/724-4160) You pays your money, you takes your chances. Inexpensive.

RESTAURANTS

Ajili Mojili (6 Clemenceau at Joffre) Most "in" place to savor Puerto Rican cuisine. Nice.

Augusto's (in Hotel Excelsior, 801 Ponce de Leon Avenue) Award-winning Austrian food, Continental fare; currently *the* upscale haunt in P.R.

Compostela (106 Condado Avenue) Classic Spanish treats, with some of the best seafood in town.

Don Juan (in San Juan Hotel) Perenial high-priced favorite. Not trendy, but always attracts an elegant crowd.

El Zipperle (352 FDR Avenue, Hato Rey) A happy marriage of Spanish and German cuisines. Longtime favorite of tourists and locals alike.

La Rotisserie (in Caribe Hilton Hotel) Probably San Juan's best known bastion of *haute cuisine francaise.* Pricey.

La Tasca (54 Munoz Rivera Avenue) Scrumptuous seafood in downscale surroundings (though not as cheap as it should be, given its site).

Lotus Flower (in Condado Plaza Hotel) One of the world's best Chinese restaurants, sez *New York Times.* And they're right.

Maria's (204 Cristo St.) Happening Mexican eatery in the center of Old San Juan. Young and hip.

Normandie Restaurant (in Radisson Normandie

Hotel) Expensive French fare in landmark hotel. Quiet and romantic.

Yuki Yu (311 Recinto Sur) Trendy sushi bar (every city needs one).

SHOPPING

In case you hadn't realized, San Juan doesn't really rank with Paris and Milan. In fact, unless you're a shopaholic, there's no reason to search out shops. Only two, in fact, merit special mention. One is Nono Maldonado, San Juan's best known designer, whose shops are on Ashford Avenue (next to the Ramada) and in the tony San Juan Hotel in Isla Verde. Nono, former fashion editor for *Esquire* magazine, creates two lines a year for women and men; his creations are upbeat and classic, though far from cheap. (He complements his wares with hand-picked bests from other clothing lines.) The other store to visit is Eva Sol y Luna in Old San Juan—Stevie Nicks would frequent this joint if she were in town: lacy and beaded oddities that look great with 6-inch boots.

Plaza Las Americas is the largest mall in Latin America, but except for sociological value (it attracts the entire metropolitan island, rich and poor), there's not much to note. National chains meet flashy Latin duds. Go if you're bored. There are also some decent boutiques in

Old San Juan, but again, you'll find mostly mainland clothing lines—nothing to shout about.

NIGHTLIFE

Clubs

As one trendy local put it, "We go out every night, but the places aren't very good." With that proviso in mind, the choices are:

Amadeus (in El San Juan Hotel) extends the Teutonic composer name-theme, though God knows why. At present, the toniest disco crowd in town.

Amadeus Café Restaurant (106 San Sebastian) It is certainly the trendiest place in town, for whatever that's worth. Crowded from early evening on.

Juliana's (in Caribe Hilton) formerly King Disco, now second (at least) to Amadeus. Worth a look-see if you're Hilton-bound.

Las Violetas. Quasi-interesting pre-disco bar.

Lazer (251 Cruz) One of Old San Juan's busiest night-spots, with (self-proclaimed) "best light show in P.R." (Go if you like; even as a child, I found the Hayden Planetarium a crashing bore.)

Peggy Sue (1 R.H. Todd) Smallish bar/disco, tepid '50s theme. Very young.

Tropix (154 San Justo) Trendy outlet in Old San Juan: café/gallery/pub. With Amadeus, your surest bet.

Gay

Bachelor Club (112 Avenida Condado) *Número uno*, though '70s high disco motif is pretty lame. Cha cha cha.

Seaview (at Atlantic Beach Hotel) is a (somewhat) picturesque oceanfront bar. Happy hour best. Gay gringos and muchachas (all of whom look and sound like Bette Midler).

ST. LOUIS

If St. Louis was notable for anything during the '70s, it was as a goal post of urban decay. In perhaps no city except Detroit was white flight so evident and the city core so grossly underused.

Wonder of wonders: today, all that's changed. Like Baltimore, St. Louis has taken long and strident steps toward reversing the fortunes of its downtown; if slightly less than bustling, central St. Louis has been revitalized beyond recognition of its former self.

The erection of the Gateway Arch was certainly a strongly symbolic first step. Photographs make this magnificent structure look like little more than a misplaced

McDonald's arch; but in person, it is a shimmering landmark that deserves the city's pride.

Designed by Finnish-American architect Eero Saarinen, it is far more than the two-dimensional figure you may think it to be. Remarkable for its height alone (it is taller than the Washington Monument, for one), the curve of its parabola is emphasized by a texture that seemingly changes with the time of day. By day, the surface appears to be matte-like; at night, the Arch glitters and glows. (Dusk, by the way, is the best time to travel to its top; the view of the surrounding region is commanding indeed.)

This may sound hyperbolic, but you'll change your mind upon seeing the Arch first-hand, a sighting that's enhanced by the vast expanse of the Mississippi below. Trust me on this one.

Not far from the Arch lies Laclede's Landing, another hallmark of the redevelopment plan. It's a standard creation of the South Street Seaport/Inner Harbor type (i.e., tourists and yuppies abound) but one should be grateful for the landing's positive effect on St. Louis' urban scene. Along with the St. Louis Centre Mall, it has certainly brought the crowds back downtown.

Natives will harp on their self-proclaimed sophistication vis-à-vis Kansas City, and this is probably a statement of fact—though Paris, this ain't. In terms of culture, however, St. Louis would do any city proud. The palatially stunning Art Museum in Lafayette Park is among the best in the United States, and the collection of works by German Expressionists is especially strong. As you'd imagine, the museum is also home to excellent traveling exhibits as well. The Symphony Orchestra is also quite impressive. It's certainly among the ten best in America.

The avant-garde arts are not as well represented (though one might predict a gallery movement in neo-chic Soulard, the south of downtown). The Central West End is not only one of the prettiest sections of town, but also one that houses most of St. Louis's affluent young residents. It is certainly my favorite area of town. You can spend a lot of time just strolling Euclid Avenue, the neighborhood's main drag.

Don't fail to take a rest at Café Balaban, the hippest such place in town. It's a de facto home base to the artsy/wanna-be set, and the food happens to be rather good. You're sure to find a hip-looking crowd of folks who are bound to know what's going on later that night. Another good bet is Bar Italia, a *molto Milanese* café with pasta, gelato, and a thoroughly Mediterranean staff.

Baseball is big news in St Louis; be forewarned that people will assume you share the fascination with them. No, St. Louis isn't the most glamorous spot on earth, but it's a fine symbol of success—as a solidly redeveloped American city with nice folks and heartland charm. There's something very reassuring in that.

IN TRANSIT

TWA is the way to go. It has more flights to the St. Louis hub than does any other carrier. It should be your first choice. Whatever your feelings about Mr.

Icahn, TWA has improved its service to a very com-
petitive degree and is definitely an airline you should
want to check out "wherever your final destination
may be."

GETTING CENTERED

St. Louis, like most provincial cities, is expansive
and can be covered best by car. Given the low price
of taxis, this mode of transport is a worthwhile alternative—though it's no cinch hailing a cab on the
street, and waits tend to be long.

The newly renovated downtown is a good place to
start, and most large hotels are found here. The city core
is easily covered by foot, though other than the Arch and
Laclede's Landing, the touristy redeveloped area on the
Mississippi mentioned earlier, there's not much to do or
see.

To the south of downtown is Soulard, a working-class
district increasingly settled by the yuppie trade. Park
Avenue is the main drag, and several trendy eateries line
the streets. To Soulard's west is tony Lafayette Park, one
of the prime addresses in town. You can admire the
stately townhomes here but there's little of interest to do.

Farther west is the lovely Central West End, where
the young and trendy congregate and live. The main
artery of the West End is Euclid Avenue, and it is
appropriately lined by chichi restaurants and stores.
More than anywhere else in St. Louis, it is a fine place to
café-sit, have lunch, and whittle away the day.

Finally, to the city's northwest is University City, home of Washington University, the most prestigious college in town, and the only one with a national reputation of note. Though you'll really need a car (or high cab budget) to get out there, you should make the trip—not so much for the shopping, which is sparse, but for the several excellent restaurants on Delmar Boulevard, the town's main street. (Saleem's and La Patisserie are the keynotes here.)

And there you have it. The city's spread out, but since there are only a few areas to cover, you should be able to see everything without any trouble at all.

HOTELS

Adam's Mark (Fourth and Chestnut; 314/741-2000) The city's best large hotel, right across from the Arch. Many great views. Drawback: middlebrow, conventioneering crowd. Expensive.

Chase Park Plaza (212 N. Kings Highway; 314/361-2500) Recently renovated grand hotel, a throwback to the city's glory days. Close enough to trendy Central West End and downtown; thus, a very wise choice. High moderate.

Forest Park Hotel (4910 W. Pine Blvd; 314/361-3500) The only hotel right in the Central West End, thus one you should consider. It's huge but more than a little dowdy, though a renovation is being planned. Excellent retro-diner downstairs. Inexpensive.

Holiday Inn Riverfront (200 N. Fourth St.; 314/621–8200) Typical HI property, enhanced by proximity to Laclede's Landing and Arch. A reasonable, if less than elegant, choice. High moderate.

Majestic Hotel (1019 Pine; 314/436–2355) St. Louis's classiest hotel, small, European ambience. Most rooms are suites, exquisitely appointed ones at that. *The* place to stay. Very expensive.

Motel 6 Northeast (1405 Dunn Road; 314/869–9400) Calling David Lynch: what lurks behind closed doors? Dirt-cheap inn for roadsters and perverts alike. Inexpensive.

RESTAURANTS

Bar Italia (4656 Maryland) Very trendy, rather authentic Italian bar/cafe with pasta king. A must!

Burrito Brothers (6600 Delmar) Funky, informal Mexican spot on University City's main drag.

Café Balaban (405 N. Euclid) Hippest Café/restaurant in town. A local institution and must-go.

Café Zoe (1923 Park Ave.) Chic little eatery in Soulard. The best of the lot on this nabe's new restaurant row.

California Do-Nut (2924 S. Jefferson) Campiest neon

sign in town, pure '40s memorabilia. Have a 'nut and a cuppa java here!

Cardwell's (8100 Maryland) Haut-yuppie restaurant rated #2 in town by *St. Louis* magazine. Food is really quite good.

Cunnetto House of Pasta (5453 Magnolia) Prima pasta on Hill. (Like other neighborhood places, it's not trendy, but go for the food.)

Duff's (392 S. Euclid) Hamburgers, readings, etc. Quasi-boho outlet, always crowded.

Eat Rite (622 Chouteau and other locations) Another kitsch spot with best swivel stools in town. $1.40 burger is the thinnest in the Western World. Wait staff a scream!

Empanada's (32 N. Euclid) The name says it all. Trendy little spot in trendy Central West End.

Forest Park Deli (4910 West Pine) In bottom of Forest Park Hotel, a kitschy retro deli with great diner fare.

Giovanni's (5201 Shaw) Arguably the best (and priciest) Italian eatery on the Hill, St. Louis' Italian neighborhood, with decor and service as you'd expect.

Lafayette Gourmet & Café (1915 Park Ave.) A take-out gourmet shop cum small dining room; a fine place for quick and solo bites.

La Patisserie (6269 Delmar) Funkiest spot in town; student/boho eatery with eclectic fare. Great brunch spot in University City.

La Veranda (in Drury Inn Hotel) Italian/Nouvelle by locally renowned chef. New, but looks to be trendy spot.

Matteo's (7491 Big Bend Blvd.) Italian café is trendy, though nouvelle, too-pink, restaurant is not. It's time, given new menu, to change Italian name, folks.

Patty Long's (1931 Park Ave.) Light fare, pleasant surroundings in Soulard.

Redel's (310 Debaliviere) You can imagine how they butcher the name of the street. They butcher most of the food, too, though it remains a very popular lunch and dinner spot. Tepid Southwestern influence.

Red Sea (6511 Delmar) Premier Ethiopian outlet, inexpensive and very good.

Ricardo's Italian Café (2001 Park Ave.) Popular lunch spot in Soulard, specializing in pasta and other light Italian fare. Very pretty, too.

Riddle's Penultimate Café (6307 Delmar) Eclectic/nouvelle menu, with varying results, full of local-trendy crowd. A good value for a dinner out.

Rigazzi's (4945 Daggett) Beer out of fishbowls. For bowlers and kids. Cheap.

Saleem's (6501 Delmar) Lebanese fare in University City; very authentic service and decor. A fine spot indeed.

Sundecker's (900 N. 1st) Laclede's Landing favorite.

More than a trifle yupped-out, but lovely sundeck overlooking the Mississippi makes up for that.

Sunshine Inn (8 1/2 S. Euclid) Healthwise eatery that (thank God) now serves chicken and fish. Cute and informal.

Tony's (826 N. Broadway) One of nine five-star Mobil Guide Restaurants in the States. Always rated #1; reserve far in advance. Innovative Italian cuisine.

SHOPPING

As you might have expected, St. Louis is no shopping mecca, but there are a couple of fun places to spend some extra time. And others, to wit:

Central West End, centered on Euclid Avenue, is the funky/trendy area, with antique, book and record stores, vintage shops, and more. The best fashion spots are Zigi and Venus Adonis, arguably the hippest games in town.

Laclede's Landing on the Mississippi, is probably best avoided—touristy doodads that will make you scream. Too bad, since the setting is picturesque enough.

Plaza Frontenac is the most elite suburban mall with faux-colonial decor. Saks, Neiman's, Gucci, Bruno Magli, et al. If you need a dress for a cotillion, this is where to go.

St. Louis Centre features the two largest local department stores, Dillard's and Famous Barr; the other stores slant downscale. Worth a quick look-see when you're downtown; this mall helped revitalize St. Louis' core.

Union Square is worth a visit for its magnificent renovation, though the mainstream mall tenants may leave you cold. Do see the Grand Lounge, in the Hyatt Regency, with a gilded dome that is nothing short of majestic—it once housed the largest railroad station in the U.S.

University City's Delmar Boulevard has a few interesting used-record shops and such, and merits a look-see if you have some (very) extra time.

NIGHTLIFE

Clubs

St. Louis is not a nightlife mecca; there are a few cool spots, and the rest are tacky as hell. Your guide:

Casa Loma Ballroom (3354 Iowa) A very mixed and odd bag: orchestra alternates big-band and top-40 sounds. Oldster and young funkster crowd.

Harpo's (928 N. 1st) Popular yuppie Laclede's Landing bar. Got it?

Kennedy's (612 N. 2nd) The crowd's the pits, but this Landing spot sometimes has nationally known alternative bands. Up to you.

Mississippi Nights (914 N. 1st) Quasi-known bands, some experimental. Check the guide to see who's playing and ignore the crowd.

Oz (300 Monsanto in Sauget, IL) On Sundays, the alternative crowd meets here. And so should you. Hip-hop, house sounds roar!

Rupert's (5130 Oakland) Mainstream, young crowd; branch of Minneapolis club. A last resort.

1227 (1227 Washington) Alternative, postpunk music and crowd. Mixed, upbeat clientele; one of the few truly cool places in town.

Zone 8 (75 Maryland Plaza) Young, trendy crowd. Owner is gay, but locals say rejects openly gay couples. If hypocrites are your thing, check out the scene.

Gay

Faces (East St. Louis) Ignore slayings in parking lot and check out this Illinois hothouse. Disco, piano bar, sex lounge, and more. Crowd ranges from gay and straight trendies to transvestites—must be seen to be believed!

Magnolia (5 S. Vandeventer) Unfashionable crowd,

ramshackle decor. Go for a hoot at the hinterlands clientele. Hee-haw!

Twist Lounge (1224 Washington) *The* hip gay hotspot; black, warehouse-y look and great house/progressive sounds. Women welcome.

TORONTO

At some point in the '70s, Toronto passed Montreal as Canada's largest metropolitan area. And while it still has a way to go to usurp the latter's European charms, Toronto is a thriving, commercially powerful city that bustles along at a heady pace.

I've always considered Toronto the Canadian Chicago, and locals have in fact borrowed the phrase "the city that works." And that it does: public services are excellent, the standard of living is high, and natives put on near-perpetually happy faces. Unlike Chicago, however, Toronto boasts one of the lowest crime rates of any metropolis in the industrialized world.

Toronto's relative factor of safety derives in no small

part from its demographic tableau. The most sociologically diverse of Canada's cities, it fosters ethnic identity—Toronto's neighborhoods are frequently defined by their residents' country of origin—while encouraging assimilation into the Canadian way of life. Chief among this is a strong work ethic, owing primarily to the city's strong English/Protestant roots. Certainly, the city's educational system is strong, and the work force—in direct contrast to that of New York's—is prepared to cope with the high-tech, idea-driven workplace in which we live.

In the same vein, Toronto's ethnic groups coexist in a harmony that American cities would benefit from. Toronto, even more than New York, continues to attract immigrants seeking a "land of opportunity" in which they can measurably improve their lives. (Let it here be said that Canada's immigration policy is more liberal than our own, though that in itself should not reflect poorly on American policy; in a country geographically larger than ours, with one-tenth of our population, the Canadians need people.)

Most importantly, émigrés come to Canada to work. So the oft-discussed Canadian welfare net exists, but to a tiny degree compared with the British dole or America's welfare state. "Doing for oneself" is very much the Canadian frame of mind!

Hearkening back to the Chicago analogy, Toronto, too, has a reputation for being rather staid—especially by those freewheelin' Latins in Montreal! Bars do close at 1:00 A.M. (sometimes later on weekends), and locals regularly rue the unenergetic nightlife scene. ("With the early closing time," one Torontonian sighed, "going out is over almost before it's begun.") Yet take heart: there are a couple of happening places—none of that critical nightlife blues.

Only recently has Toronto become a fashion city, and it still lags behind Frenchy-chic Montreal. But one would be remiss to bypass happening Queen Street West, one of the funkiest and most avant-garde shopping streets in the world—though the centuries-old preppy standard continues to dominate Toronto's sartorial scene. (One also sees this look in Montreal, though it's the European neo-preppy style, always a shade more butt-hugging and funked-up there.)

To be a total charmer, a city should have a unique and unified style of architecture, and Toronto misses the mark by a wide margin here. In fact, I'd be hard-pressed to describe the ruling edificial class; even tony Yorkville is marked by undistinguished, early-'70s mid-rise apartment houses, and little more. You won't find New York's prewar style, Miami's Art Deco, San Francisco's Victorian. Toronto instead is a mixed architectural bag.

In a way, it's too bad that Toronto doesn't dazzle, because it would be heartening to find a city that has it all. But what it does have—superfriendly natives, urban safety, and much to see, eat, and do—may, in the end, be quite enough.

One final note: Toronto is not a city to be visited in the winter months. Though less frigid than Montreal, it's pretty damn cold, and unless you dig spending all your time indoors, you'd better wait till summer to come.

IN TRANSIT

Air Canada's new fleet of airbuses make whisking off to Toronto a snap. Even on the shortest of flights, the in-flight staff make your trip a special pleasure indeed—and on longer flights, you can count on multiplying the charm.

You can fly to Toronto directly on Air Canada from the following cities in the United States: New York (La Guardia and Newark), Boston, Miami, Tampa, Chicago, Los Angeles, and San Francisco.

GETTING CENTERED

Metropolitan Toronto is vast and huge, actually comprised of six municipalities—but don't get put off. Central Toronto is more than manageable, laid out in a sensible grid, and easily traveled by a superclean, ultraefficient Metro. There's an excellent bus system, too.

Here's a quick guide to the neighborhoods that will interest you. Starting at the south, there's Lake Ontario, which provides much summer pleasure, especially at the Beaches district. A couple of blocks north, on Front Street, is Union Station, representing the base of downtown.

A couple of blocks east is Yonge Street, billed as "the longest street in the world." (It goes off somewhere into the Canadian wilds after leaving town.) Yonge serves as the main north-south artery of town.

Proceeding north up Yonge, you'll soon hit Queen Street. To the left is ultratrendy Queen Street West, with the most happening shops and restaurants in town.

About a kilometer up the road, you'll hit Wellesley Street. This is the heart of the popular yuppie and gay area that has many wonderful restaurants, pubs, and other places to hang. Another half a kilometer uptown past Bloor and Yonge, is Yorkville Avenue, the toniest upscale shopping street in town (though not nearly as modern and funky as Queen Street West). Formerly a boho colony, it's now a place to live and be seen.

And those are the areas in which you're likely to spend most of your time. Hopefully, you'll have a friend with a car who can show you around to the rest of Toronto's vast expanse as well.

HOTELS

Amsterdam Guest House (209 Carlton St.; 416/921-9797) Elegant little Victorian, also very central. A lovely place to stay, for a song. Moderate.

Beaches Bed & Breakfast (174 Waverley Road; 416/699-0818) Delightful private home in the Beaches, about 20 minutes from downtown; a perfect summer choice. Inexpensive.

Bond Place (65 Dundas St. East; 416/392-6061) Comfortable, basic hotel with great downtown location. Inexpensive.

Guild Inn (201 Guildwood Parkway; 416/261-3331) Relaxing inn atop Scarborough Bluffs, overlooking Lake Ontario. Huge grounds include gardens and historical architecture, with sculpture galore. Quite nice. Expensive.

Hotel Ibis (240 Jarvis St.; 416/593-9400) Scandinavian design and great central location. Best for the price. Moderate.

Hotel Selby (592 Sherbourne St.; 416/921-3142) Lovely, refurbished Victorian hotel. Hemingway used to call this place home. Moderate.

King Edward Hotel (37 King Street East; 416/863-9700) The classically elegant Torontonian hotel, a must for the upper crust. Right in the heart of downtown. Very expensive.

Park Plaza Hotel (4 Avenue Road; 416/924-5471) Located "uptown," convenient to Bloor-Yorkville area and shops/restaurants therein. Renovated, semi-grand old hotel. Expensive.

Skydome Hotel (416/360-7100) Perhaps the most futuristic hotel in the world, a masterwork of postmodern design. Half the rooms look out onto the Skydome Stadium—a somewhat eerie view!—and ball games, concerts, or other events are yours for the asking. Very expensive.

RESTAURANTS

Auberge Gavroches (90 Avenue Rd.) Haute cuisine (and prices), yet remarkably *décontracté*. A great expense account joint.

Bellair (100 Cumberland St.) See and be seen Yorkville haunt, though not for artistes. California nouvelle menu, slightly heavy-handed decor. Outdoor garden is a decided summer scene.

Bemelman's (83 Bloor St. W) A Toronto tradition, especially after the clubs close and for Sunday brunch. I 's like any brass brunch joint, circa Manhattan '78. Still draws the crowds, including many stars. Avoid specials, stick with burgers, omelets, and such.

Bistro 990 (990 Bay St.) Deservedly happening French country cuisine, with charming auberge feeling and seasonal, ultrafresh food. Visiting film stars and celebs galore. Happening highbrow bar scene.

By the Way Café (Bloor & Brunswick) Divey, punky, vital café, one you should not miss. Open late.

Café la Gaffe (51 Kensington Ave.) Yuppified bohemia. Need I say more?

Centro (2472 Yonge) Cal-Italo menu, phosphorescent decor. Mesquite-grilled, ultrafresh fish and meat. Very trendy and very good.

4-D'S Diner (10 Bellair St.) Retro diner, nicely done, and great for solo dining. But stick to the basics here.

Grano (2035 Yonge) Traditional Northern Italian cuisine, *senza* annoying nouvelle touches. Home-baked breads and antipasti are best.

La Hacienda (649 Queen St. W) Appropriately named café, filled with local artwork, hard-core music (usually) and boho clientele.

Lakes (1112 Yonge) Nouvelle-ish menu, media/high yuppie crowd. Cute blue lakey decor.

Le Select (328 Queens St. W.) *Très nouvelle. Et très bon.* Trendy and crowded place.

Mars (432 College) Landmark greasy spoon—best high-cholesterol breakfasts in town! Supercrowded on weekends.

Metropolis (838 Yonge) Specializes in all-Canadian food (I know—good question). But it's game, rabbit, fish, and such, in a semifunky setting. Very popular, and an advised stop for you.

Natalie's House (2650 Danforth) New boho haunt recently opened by the Queen of Alternative Toronto. Looks to be an instant institution. Light fare cum café/bookstore.

Nekah (32 Wellington St. E.) Means "flying geese" in some Indian tongue. Among the top five restaurants in Canada: austere, Oriental, New Age decor, served thusly. Described as "multi-cultural Canadiana"; afterward, you may want a Big Mac.

Portobello (55 Avenue Rd.) Good basic Italian food; a nice respite from the distressingly chic.

Pronto (692 Mount Pleasant) Does no major city lack a restaurant with this name? *Non credo che si.* This one's glitzy (duh) and nouvelle, with near-psychotic flavor combinations. Big Mac time again!

Rhodes (1496 Yonge St.) The best of the lot in an uptown YP district; rather charming decor and No. American food with an oriental touch.

Rodney's Oyster House (209 Adelaide E.) Trendy seafood place. A fun upscale scene.

Rosedale Diner (1164 Yonge St.) Big portions, stick-to-the-ribs food, with modern touches. Beware: no diner prices here!

Santa Fe (131 Peter) Ultrafashionable, young crowd, Southwestern cuisine. Models, trendies, galore.

Scaramouche (1 Benvenuto) Ongoingly trendy place with classic French fare and a charming city view.

Scattered Crackers (700 King St. W.) Postmodern decor, great grilled food, less bizzarrely prepared than the surroundings would suggest.

The Boat (158 Augusta Ave.) Tasty Portuguese eatery, totally unpretentious and much fun.

The Liberty (105 Church) Ever-popular, good traditional menu, with surprising culinary flair. A classic on Toronto's dining scene.

The Other Café (483 Bloor St. W.) Burgers, pasta, etc.; casual-chic crowd. The terrace is great during warm weather.

Tidal Wave (1590 Queen St. E.) Prime sushi, with a fun touch: fishbits float to you on minirafts sent out from bar. Cute, huh?

Trapper's (3479 Yonge) Interesting neo-Canadian cuisine, especially fish. Upscale, not trendy, clientele.

SHOPPING

Toronto's shopping choices rival the most sophisticated in the world. And unlike New York, people are actually nice when you walk into a store! Prime areas are:

Bloor/Yorkville is home to the high-fashion boutiques, including top international names and local talent. Great accessories/furniture stores, as well as the heart of Toronto's gallery scene.

Eaton Centre is one of the largest in the world and is architecturally distinctive as well: the mile-high station like skylight gives an air of grandeur to the place. On Yonge between Dundas and Queen; there are more than 360 restaurants and shops.

Hazelton Lanes is an indoor complex in the heart of Yorkville, with the highest-priced boutiques in town. Skip if you don't have *mucho* loot.

Queen's Quay Terminal boasts a somewhat touristy (yet upscale) array of shops, restaurants, and boutiques. I recommend it for the gorgeous natural setting. Count on an hour or so here.

Queen Street West is the boho/avant-garde shopping street, and there's much to do and see. On a warm afternoon, you can easily make a day of lunch and shopping on Queen between University Avenue and Bathurst Street. Should be your prime stop.

Sherway Gardens, west of downtown, is most notable for its upscale food court, and not much else.

NIGHTLIFE

As said before, Toronto's nightlife is not its strong suit. If the conservative government ever extended closing time past 1:00 A.M., you could bet on a scene that would flourish in seconds flat.

Clubs

For now, the choices are:

Bamboo Club (312 Queen St. W) An institution: Thai food, reggae bands, very casual atmosphere. Avoid on weekends—very suburban crowd.

Berlin (2335 Yonge) A tarnished flower; once very

trendy, now rather suburban. Live bands sometimes worth checking out.

Big Bop (651 Queen St. W) Young rock crowd, two floors. Unrestrained fun.

Brunswick House (481 Bloor) Young postpunk crowd; bands at times.

Diamond Club (410 Sherbourne) Worth a visit for live bands; check to see what's on. Else, avoid.

Lizard (64 Gerrard St. E.) Most fun on Sundays, when it's mixed but predominantly gay.

RPM (132 Queens Quay E) A former chic spot, now home to a university (and would-be) crowd. Monday night's best.

Stilife (217 Richmond St. W.) Still #1, the city's premier alternative club. Selective entry, great '82 Manhattan decor. Dark and murky (that's a recommendation.)

Tasmanian Ballroom (101 Jarvis) House/black music, still popular for a get-down time.

PWD Dinkel's (88 Yorkville) Primarily a band scene, but sleazy enough to merit a quick visit, especially given lackluster competition.

Gay

Chaps (9 Isabella St.) Ever-popular cruise bar with Western motif.

Komrad's (1 Isabella St.) Video/dance bar with young, modern crowd.

Trax (529 Yonge St.) Huge, passé disco concept. But still packed on weekends.

VANCOUVER

Temptress Vancouver almost dares you not to fall in love.

Blessed with a harbor setting that is an unsung wonder of the world, Vancouver—like San Francisco and Rio—boasts geographical grandeur that is second to none in the world. Add to that the miraculously sympathetic natives, an embraceable climate, and a level of sophistication not normally associated with the Pacific Northwest. Canada's third-largest city is pretty much a dream come true.

Tourism is Vancouver's premier industry, and it's not hard to see why. The city seems to refresh the senses from the moment one arrives, and the mix of natural splendor and man-made fun continues to invigorate visitors throughout their stay.

Outdoorsy types could hardly ask for anything more: ski slopes are less than half an hour from downtown, Stanley Park beckons bikesters and hikesters alike, and camping is king. Trust me—it's all here and more. (Oh yes, fishing is a popular pastime, though a bit too strenuous for the likes of me.)

But even sedentary types will be lured to prowl Vancouver's streets. It's very much of a strolling city, though you'll need some form of transport to get from one neighborhood of interest to the next. (Luckily, the excellent public bus and metro systems help out in this respect.) The air quality alone fairly sings to sooty-lunged cosmopolites and sirens footly jaunts.

And another word of caution. Once the town's natural charm grabs you, expect to experience a period of calm, then a more gradual seduction. Vancouver is not a rapid-paced, high-fire city that will knock you off your feet; instead, it exerts a far more lulling lure, a vixen of the slow-but-sure sort.

Vancouver is the wealthiest city in Canada, despite its lack of a strong manufacturing base. In many ways, it represents the best of all possible worlds: a vibrant service economy that seems to perpetuate itself. Unlike New York, where much of the poorly educated populace lacks the prospect of finding post-high school industrial jobs, Vancouver's educational system prepares workers for the service economy at hand. Interestingly enough, while the city prides itself on ethnic diversity, identification with one's roots effects a mood of individual worth;

in New York, conversely, one could argue that this same attitude has resulted in the existence of a separatist underclass.

There is also a sense of history in renovated districts like Gastown, just adjacent to the city's core. And rather than being razed, old warehouses and other edifices are reclaimed for use in housing and commercial projects alike.

But that's very much in the spirit of Vancouver, a city that maintains its history with a very definite eye on the future. And let's not forget the present. Vancouver is a destination you will surely not want to let slip by!

IN TRANSIT

It's a truism that Canadians are nicer than Americans, and truisms are, after all, true. Nowhere is this more apparent than in the service provided by Air Canada, which now rates among the best in the world. In terms of service, cuisine, and ambience, you'll not find a better airline anywhere!

Air Canada offers connecting service to Vancouver from Boston, Miami, Tampa, Chicago, Los Angeles, and San Francisco. Contact your travel agent or Air Canada to determine the best route for yourself.

GETTING CENTERED

I would be remiss if I didn't advise you to stay near the harbor, which is both breathtakingly panoramic and central. If you can swing a harbor-view room at the Pan Pacific Hotel, don't give any other accommodation a second thought! (The hitch is, of course, that you may spend all day at the window and sigh; and the view is even more glorious at night!)

The harbor is at the base of downtown, to the east of which lies the historic—and newly trendy—Gastown and Chinatown districts. Granville Avenue is the main north-south artery, and staying near it will put you smack in the center of things.

Going east-west, Robson is the main drag, and a shopping/café street you'll certainly want to see. South Granville is more upscale than the area of the avenue in the middle of town, and this area of course has its share of nice hotels; it's a bit off the beaten path, but Vancouver is not huge, so not inaccessibly so.

West Vancouver, across the Burrard Inlet (aka the harbor!), is where the young professionals live, and its high-rise buildings give the area a very citified feel. There are several nice restaurants, though they're somewhat local-ish; since downtown is so close, most people end up there.

And that's pretty much it. Central Vancouver is compact and easily mastered—and that a city can pack so much into so concentrated an area speaks to its overall charm.

HOTELS

Barclay (1348 Robson St.; 688-8850) A marvelous choice: charming, Old World, right on bustling

Robson Street, for a song. Do consider this! Inexpensive.

Georgia (801 W. George St.; 682-5566) Very comfortable and central European-style hotel; the best bet for the money. Moderate.

Meridien (845 Burrard St.; 682-5511) Very luxurious and very central; but what Meridien isn't? Isabella Rossellini was staying here when I was in town—nuff said? Very expensive.

Pan Pacific (999 Canada Place; 662-8111) Supermodern palace with the best harbor view in town—and here, that means a lot. The new prime address. Very expensive.

Park Royal (440 Clyde St.; 926-5511) A lovely little hotel near up-and-coming Sixth Avenue. Cheaper than downtown hostelries, and very charming at that. Moderate.

Royal Garden (1110 Howe St.; 684-2151) A perfectly reasonable choice for a comfortable, low-cost hotel. Situated near Vancouver's club scene. Low moderate.

Sylvia (1154 Gilford St.; 681-9321) Not the most central, but attractive and unbeatable for the price. Inexpensive.

Vancouver (900 W. Georgia St.; 684-3131) The city's landmark hotel, long a favorite address. Stately, but not stuffy (this is Vancouver, remember?). Expensive.

RESTAURANTS

Art Gallery Café (in Vancouver Art Museum, Hornby & Robson) Nouvelle meals, microwaved in front of your eyes (I swear!). A semitrendy place to meet for a cheapish lunch.

Bishops (2183 W. 4th St.) Upscale crowd, top-of-the-line French. Seafood's the best bet here.

Bridge's (1696 Duranleau, on Granville Island) California-esque (read: quasi-nouvelle) menu. Very popular place for brunch, especially when the patio is in use.

Brow (Canada Place) West Coast nouvelle, top rated in town, with breathtaking harbor view. Should be your big expense-account meal or splurge.

Doll & Pennies (1167 Davie) Haut-kitsch decor, inside and out. Amazing hamburgers, all night long. Gender-bender decor attracts crowds 24 hours a day.

Hamburger Mary's (1202 Davie) Nearly as funky as the one in San Francisco. A counterculture hangout, transvestite owned and operated. Definitely a Vancouver must!

Imperial (355 Burrard) Among the finest Chinese places in North America. Exquisitely prepared food. Not your standard takeout place!

Joe Forte's (777 Thurlow) After work, yups; later at night, a trendy clientele. Classic bar and grill, brass decor; steaks and seafood the best. A Vancouver institution.

Kirin's (1166 Alberini) Upscale Chinese. Not a trendspot, but just about the best Chinese food you'll ever have. Inventive, hearty, and fine.

La Bodega Tapas Bar (1277 Howe) Not as trendy as it should be; tapas evidently aren't yet "in" out Vancouver way. But a great place for wonderful Spanish cuisine.

Milieu (1145 Robson) Haut-trendy French bistro. You know the type.

Orestes (3116 W. Broadway) Cheap, funky Greek joint. Especially busy during summer; yups in heat.

Quilicum (1724 Davie) Truly unique: Native American cuisine! (Please don't ask me to describe.) Indian wall-hangings and folkloric artifacts galore. Kind of a kick.

Shijo (1926 W. 4th St.) Postmodern decor (white with spotlights—you know the type). Probably the trendiest Japanese joint in town.

Shogun (518 Hornby) Cheap noodle shop downtown. Great for a fast solo lunch.

Sophie's Cosmic Café (2095 W. 4th) A fave spot for weekend brunch, but pretty damn cool any time of the day. The kitschy surroundings are worth a visit. Don't miss!

Tafs Café (829 Granville St.) The city's premier

postpunk café: bohos, intellectuals, and more. Light food, too, but primarily a place to hang during the day and before going out to clubs.

Umberto's Il Giardino (1362 Hornby) Visiting film stars and local luminaries are here in force. Primo Northern Italian food. In warm weather, the court-yard is a must.

Woodland's (2582 West Broadway) Is vegetarian buffet the newest dining trend? Let's hope not; still, this neighborhoody place is casual and much fun.

SHOPPING

You'll probably be dazzled by Vancouver's seemingly endless shopping possibilities. For a city its size, there are myriad prospects, ranging from super high-fashion to mass- and tourist-inspired goods. (The former are what you're after, of course.) Here's everything you need to know:

City Square on Canbie Street is a cute little city mall where you might find a funky accessory or two. If you're in the nabe; not really worth a separate trip.

Gastown, the refurbished working-class district right next to downtown, is beginning to see an explosion of avant-garde shops. While this is still a new trend, don't fail to stalk its main arteries, specifically Water and Cordova Streets. (Peter Fox Shoes are among the hippest in the world, and this Vancouver-based designer has a store here.)

Granville Island is touristy as hell, but the big, enclosed market is a lot of fun; one can make a cheap lunch out of the little food stalls and sit-down places in the back.

Oakridge Mall is the main upscale retailing giant, though it slants suburban.

Pacific Centre is a huge, mainly underground, mall featuring Dunhill, Cartier, Daniel Hechter, and their ilk. Not avant, but worth a visit for die-hard shopping fans.

Robson Street is the most-traveled shopping street in town, with a mixture of high-fashion and mass. Avoid on weekends, when suburban kids overpower everything else. The Robson Fashion Mart has Ferragamo, Ralph Lauren, and other designer duds.

Sinclair Centre, right downtown, is a charming little city mall that features Leone's, a long arcade of the trendiest duds in town; one could easily outfit oneself for the rest of one's life in the boutiques here. The Gianni Versace boutique is also here, and an Emporio Armani should be open by the time you read this. A sartorial must!

South Granville Street has some great Milan-esque boutiques, though they're frightfully expensive and not as on-the-mark as the ones in Sinclair. A favorite of the upper-middle-class. Boboli is worth seeing, though.

West Fourth Avenue in South Vancouver and West Broadway are emerging retail streets, though the shops are primarily for yuppies who make the area their home.

Westminster Key is a cutesy retail centre most notable for the SkyTram ride (about 35 minutes) that affords a great view of the city and shows what urban transportation *can* be.

NIGHTLIFE

Clubs

My tour guide, a hip young Vancouverite, spent much time apologizing for the state of the city's clubs. "In a couple of years, there will be a lot happening here," she promised. Lisa needn't have been so glum; there are already a couple of fun places where you'll mix with the city's trend-elite:

Arts Club Theatre (1585 Johnston) Jazz spot for young professional crowd, but sometimes cool for special events. Ask around.

Club Soda (1055 Howe) is more a dance bar, hosting local and semiknown bands. Fun and without attitude.

Fiasco's (2486 Bayswater) Restaurant/nightspot catering to mixed bag, somewhat yuppish, crowd. Thursday is the coolest night to go. Standard disco scene.

Graceland (1250 Richards) Arguably the hippest scene in town; all-black fashion victims galore. Mixed crowd, great progressive sounds. Your first stop.

Luv-A-Ffair (1275 Seymour) Fun alternative crowd on Tuesdays; other times, suburban kids have infiltrated this former #1-cool club. You know when to go.

Richards on Richards (1036 Richards). Also known as Dicks on Dicks (yes). Yuppie meat market. But the most popular one in town!

Roxy (932 Granville St.) Very young, all-in-black, postpunk crowd. Local bands, usually.

Saturno Supper Club (1320 Richards) At present, this place hosts performers like Gladys Knight, and has as its clientele kids on dates. But there's a rumor a new owner will make this well-designed spot a place to go. Check when you roll into town.

Gay

Gandy Dancer (1222 Hamilton) Fun little place with quasi-upscale gay crowd.

WASHINGTON, D.C.

Under the best of circumstances, it's a tricky proposition to write about your home town. But since I fled to New York as soon as college rolled around and returned only sporadically since then, I think I've distanced myself enough to provide an objective city view.

People tend to hate or love D.C. The former camp finds the city provincial and dull, refusing to see any redeeming qualities from the forest of government-worker drones. (Nothing is drearier than a federal job; the drab green desks and olive walls are enough to make anyone with a soupçon of style jump off the Key Bridge. This is Kafkaesque conformity at its worst. Besides, what's the point of working nine to five without Italian office furniture and a fat expense account?)

Devotees, however, laud Washington's grand-scale avenues, cozy neighborhoods, and (somewhat) varied cultural life. Remember, the Kennedy Center, Smithsonian Institution, and Arena Stage are all here.

The nation's capital's most vital—and distressing—role may be to provide a metaphor for the less-than-united state of the State. Washington is not the only American city with so vast a schism between rich and poor; but the presence of the Congress near the Anacostia ghetto makes it all the more abject. Capitol Hill itself has raised most of its tenements to accommodate faux-federal yuppie townhouse developments; in addition to providing bedroom housing for the bow-tie brigade, it precludes *Life* and *Newsweek* editors running photographs of lean-tos in the shadow of the Capitol's dome. In any case, a mayor indicted for crack smoking is not what a city with polarized race relations and the highest homicide rate in the United States needs right now.

And it doesn't take an Ed.D. to see that D.C.'s schools are a major force—of inertia—in maintaining the status quo. While the public educational institutions in the affluent Maryland and Virginia suburbs are constantly lauded by the national press, inner-city schools are woefully discredited. To Europeans, these societal inequities do not go unnoticed, and every Canadian I've ever introduced to D.C. seems appalled.

However, since the ghettos have successfully been geographically isolated, the casual visitor to D.C. probably won't see them at all. What you will see are the national monuments and heartbreakingly lovely residential neighborhoods that rank as the most architecturally charming in the land.

Washington is not a high-energy city; the low activity level of government offices seems to spill over into public life. In fact, a weekend in D.C. can be as calming as a weekend at a Caribbean resort (at least if one lives in New York!). As you might imagine, the best time to visit is spring (for the cherry blossoms on the Tidal Basin) or in fall (when the city is covered with fallen leaves). Take it from someone who has mowed more than a few lawns in D.C.'s summer heat: there are few cities as onerous as D.C. in July. Winter, however, is milder here than it is in the Northeast, and not a bad time to visit at all.

Our capital city was designed by French master planner Pierre L'Enfant, and the majesty of Paris's *grands boulevards* is much in evidence here. In terms of sheer grandeur, no other American city comes close. So, while many of the monuments and museums are clustered in the same general area of downtown, there's still a fair amount of walking you'll have to do. But, tourist buses can get you where you're going—cheaply and with ease.

Washington's museums would do any capital proud; the National Gallery, Portrait Gallery, and the Hirschhorn are the most impressive. But don't miss the charming Phillips Collection off Dupont Circle, a former mansion studded with Post-impressionist and Impressionist art. And the Smithsonian's massive museums are packed with exhibits of natural and scientific awe.

Yet D.C.'s most thrilling sights are the Capitol Building, the Washington Monument, and the Jefferson Memorial, especially at night. The latter is amazing when seen lighted against a pitch-black sky. Every nation needs its symbols. Well these are ours—and fine ones they are.

By now, you're probably singing "The Star Spangled Banner" and clutching Nancy Reagan's *My Turn* firmly to your breast. If you can momentarily break away from this patriotic frenzy, you can discover Washington's other salient points.

While the city is no bastion of the avant-garde, you'll find enough to keep you busy for at least a couple of days. Bohemia is primarily provided by the city's student population; those seriously interested in being modern boys or girls tend to go elsewhere (yes, New York) fast. When I was a lad, Dupont Circle was the hippie haven (as was Georgetown, to a lesser degree), and it still has its funky/holistic bent, but most of that scene has now moved to Adams-Morgan, the new "alternative" nabe. Centered around 17th Street and Columbia Road N.W., this district boasts more Ethiopian restaurants per square inch than, perhaps, Addis Ababa itself.

Much has been made of the Adams-Morgan phenomenon (*Washingtonian* magazine needs *something* to write about other than the Mayor's predilections); but, truth be told, it's really a very small scene. One Friday night, my friend Mike (the "punk doctor") took me to a couple of the neighborhood's hipper haunts, each of which was scantily scattered with the expected postpunk brigade. (You know, those "artsy" folks, like me, who shun the plastic "discos" of secondary towns for a dark room and old Morrissey tapes.) Similarly, the art scene in Washington tends to be both staid and small.

That said, you don't go to D.C. to party, but to enjoy the city's more cultured charms. And in the end, a little museum-hopping, shopping, and eating restaurants never hurt anyone, right?

GETTING CENTERED

Divided into four quadrants, D.C. is one of the country's most easily navigated towns. Just remember to note whether the address you seek is N.W., N.E., S.W., or S.E., or you could really get lost.

The weekend visitor will spend most of his or her time in the N.W. quadrant, which contains Georgetown, Adams-Morgan, Dupont Circle, and the elite residential district called Far Northwest. The Northeast is primarily working-class residential; the Southwest contains the waterfront, some monuments, and clubs (the plastic discos cited above); and the Southeast comprises both gentrified Capitol Hill and downtrodden Anacostia.

Neighborhoods to note:

Adams-Morgan. The neighborhood whose core is at Columbia Road N.W. between 18th and Kalorama Park is *the* zone for the terminally cool and wanna-bes. Formerly, an all-Latin ghetto, it now draws hip young

Washingtonians with its lively mixture of ethnic restaurants, shops, and clubs.

Capitol Hill. Home to young professionals, it is centered around Pennsylvania Avenue and 2nd St. S.E. Other than the Capitol Building,however, there's not much of interest here.

Connecticut Avenue. The Champs-Elysees of Washington, it is definitely one of the city's—and country's—most aristocratic avenues. As you travel uptown toward Maryland, the Old-World apartment buildings are worth a look.

Downtown. Bounded by H & K Streets, Constitution Avenue, and the Mall, D.C. has one of the world's most imposing centers. And it rolls up its carpets after dark, press releases to the contrary. A revamping of the major department stores has brought some renewed life to commercial downtown, but during post-business hours, it's a pretty sorry sight.

Dupont Circle. Now fashionably bohemian, it's an area that starving artists can no longer afford. Some of D.C.'s most beautiful Victorian rowhouses can be found here.

Georgetown. Centered at Wisconsin Avenue and M St. N.W., Georgetown still contains the District's most upscale and sought-after addresses. The Federal townhouses deserve a special look-see. Unfortunately, the neighborhood's shopping and nightlife are no longer as exclusive as they once were.

HOTELS

Adams Inn (1744 Lanier Place; 202/745-3600) The logical choice for Adams-Morgan. It's cozy, homey, and cheap. No frills—*and* no smoking. Inexpensive.

Braxton Hotel (1440 Rhode Island Ave., N.W.; 202/237-7800) Lovely little inn; a great place to stay near Dupont Circle (for a song). Inexpensive.

Capitol Hilton (16 St. between K & and L; 202/393-1000) Great name! An excellent downtown address. Newly renovated, it's almost a self-contained site, meeting every tourist's needs. Expensive.

Georgetown Dutch Inn (1075 Thos. Jefferson St. N.W.; 202/337-0900) Near the C & O Canal, a homey hotel of suites where many actors stay. The restaurant, Leo & Linda's, is top-notch. High moderate.

Hotel Anthony (1823 L St., N.W.; 202/223-4320) is a pleasant, very central hotel that's less costly than others nearby. Moderate.

Jefferson (1200 16th St. N.W.; 202/347-2200) A luxurious "boutique" where many of the rich and famous have stayed. Sumptuous furnishings (eclectic, yet on the mark) a top-rated restaurant, and ever-helpful staff. One of the country's finest. Very expensive.

Marbury Hotel (3000 M St., N.W.; 202/726-5000). Gorgeous old Georgetown property right in the middle of things. Very nice. High moderate.

Mayflower (1127 Connecticut Ave., N.W.; 202/347-3000) Perhaps Washington's most legendary hotel; political history looms in every elegant hall. Very expensive.

Ritz-Carlton (2100 Massachusetts Ave., N.W.; 202/293-2100) High-English chintz decor, international clientele. Top of the line. Very expensive.

State Plaza Hotel (2117 E St., N.W.; 202/861-8200) Another "suite" hotel, perfect for longer stays. Near Kennedy Center. Moderate.

RESTAURANTS

Because Washington isn't a fashion town, it follows that there wouldn't be a glittering dining scene. But there's still a lot of good food to be had. (And since you're not concerned with making an appearance, who cares if you eat like a hog?) The following are my favorites, but don't forget also to shop around Adams-Morgan for a cheap little ethnic place to call your own.

Au Pied Du Cochon (1335 Wisconsin Ave., N.W.) is an informal and lively bistro with *troquet* basics at prices anyone can afford. A good breakfast bet, too.

Café Splendide (1521 Connecticut Ave.) A very *gemütlich*—and embraceably inexpensive—Austrian cafe. Portions are copious, food very good. Especially nice for weekend brunch.

Cities (2424 18th St., N.W.) Adams-Morgan restaurant/club with changing-theme cuisine. (Even the decor is redone to reflect the country of the month.) One of D.C.'s most adventurous and trendiest places to eat.

Duke Zeibert's (1050 Connecticut Ave., N.W.) Not trendy, but a classic steak and potatoes joint for journalists, sports figures, and their ilk. Worth a visit for local color value. (Oat bran enthusiasts need not apply.)

Jockey Club (2100 Massachusetts Ave., N.W.) Politicos, press types galore. A D.C. institution for years. English club design, Continental fare. Pricey.

Kramerbooks & Afterwords (1517 Connecticut Ave., N.W.) Reminiscent of the Dupont Circle of my youth: artsy, cozy, posthippie cool. Still one of the most popular places in town for desserts, light meals, and conversation. Slightly precious concept, but one of the few semicafés in town, so who cares?

Le Lion D'Or (1150 Connecticut Ave., N.W.) Washington's answer to Lutece: nationally renowned French haute cuisine. *Très, très cher!*

Old Ebbitt Grill (675 15th St., N.W.) One of my favorite restaurants in the world. (Call me sentimental—I went there the night of my senior prom.) A woodsy, gorgeous old standard with Maryland seafood—the best in the world! An absolute knockout.

Red Sea (2463 18th St., N.W.) On Adams-Morgan's

famed Ethiopian row, and probably the best of the lot. Reasonably priced, funky/ethnic decor, and very animated indeed. (Ethiopian food is eaten by hand, so bring a bib if you're klutzy like me.)

Sholl's Cafeteria (1990 K St., N.W.) Should be proclaimed a national landmark. Great Southern food at pre-War prices (and the pies are a must!). Yummy breakfasts, too. Not to be missed under any circumstances!

SHOPPING

Devotees of the avant-garde will have trouble outfitting themselves here; for less trendy shoppers—especially those into preppy chic—there is lots to buy here. The major shopping districts are:

Downtown is where the department store grande dames remain. A fine reminder of what downtown shopping used to be. Of these, Garfinckel's is the most prestigious; Woodward & Lothrop is also very nice; and the new Hecht's is bright and moderately priced.

Georgetown offers the highest concentration of high-fashion goods, though lately some tacky stores and national chains have moved in. Georgetown Park is a very tony and well-designed (if ever-so-precious) urban mall, proffering a plethora of pricy boutiques.

Union Station is worth a visit for its gorgeous renovation—a landmark restored! Shops tend toward the touristy, but for their part in this important urban project, they deserve kudos here.

Upper Connecticut Avenue features Saks, Lord & Taylor, and the like.

In addition to Georgetown Park, the Mazza Gallerie is another upscale mall, located at 5300 Wisconsin Avenue N.W. And White Flint, in the Kensington-North Bethesda area, is the most opulent of the suburban malls—they even have a Bloomingdale's!

Finally, two ultratouristy downtown malls are the Pavilion at the Old Post Office and Shops at National Place. The former boasts interesting architecture and annoying gift shops (though, I suppose, the Washington Monument phallic memorabilia do rank as camp); the latter hosts all the usual mall suspects (including those marvelous national book chains that sell my craft!)

NIGHTLIFE

Washington's nightlife is just what you'd expect it to be in a city of bureaucrats: generally, a crashing bore. One of my friends comes up to New York every weekend just to hit the clubs.

Fueled by government workers and preppies, D.C.'s after-dark scene offers little of interest to the rest of us. The only real energy comes from students—Georgetown, George Washington, Catholic, and Howard Universities, most of all—and the bohemians/aging hippies, who call Dupont Circle and Adams-Morgan home.

But don't despair! Since you'll probably only be visiting D.C. for a couple of days, there's enough to keep you night owls hooting for that long. To wit:

Bars

Bradshaw's Club & Café (2319 18th St., N.W.) Nondescript bar/restaurant attracting varied Adams-Morgan crowd. An unimposing, homey place to land.

Fox & Hounds Lounge (1537 17th St., N.W.) Accepts Bradshaw's overflow. Similarly uncommitted (i.e., no) decor, but a good jukebox and cheap drinks.

Clubs

Barbecued Iguana (P St. and 13th St., N.W.) After-hours weekend haunt: very late; the coolest boys and girls in town end up here. Consult locals re special parties.

Cities (2424 18th St., N.W.) Highly mixed clientele—a happy melding of races, ages, and sexual preferences. Probably D.C.'s most popular, if slightly less than cutting edge, club.

Dakota's (1777 Columbia Rd., N.W.) Reasonably hip Adams-Morgan haunt; house music rules. (Sundays and Wednesdays are gay.)

DC Space (443 7th St., N.W.) The city's bastion of

hip—a huge performance/club complex featuring local and (sometimes) nationally known bands. Plus art, dance, and more. Not an inexpensive proposition, but definitely worth a trip.

Fifth Column (915 F St., N.W.) New York–inspired gallery/club, trashed out decor. Best during the week. D.C.'s black-clad crowd drinks here.

930 Club (930 F St., N.W.) Primarily a band showcase, but also boasts a dance floor and progressive DJ. A staple of D.C.'s underground scene.

The Vault (911 F St., N.W.) Former bank turned alternative disco. College-y, not as hip as places cited above.

Tracks (800 M St., S.E.) Mixed disco (gay/straight), open very late. *Très* '70s motif (yawn).

Gay

Badlands (1415 22 St., N.W.) Large gay meeting place; forgo '70s dance floor for dark video bar.

Clubhouse (1296 Upshur St., N.W.) Saturday only, open till 8 A.M. Mixed, very funky crowd; you can guess what ends up here at dawn.

JR's (1519 17th St., N.W.) Crowded from afternoon on. Cheap drinks, animated Dupont Circle crowd.

LOST & FOUND (56 L St., S.E.) A Washington institution *cum* suburban, '70s-inspired crowd. Thus, at your own risk.